PHILOSOPHIES OF JUSTICE IN ACHOLI

WORLD PHILOSOPHIES

Bret W. Davis, D. A. Masolo, and
Alejandro Vallega, editors

PHILOSOPHIES OF JUSTICE IN ACHOLI

Responsibility in Times of Collective Suffering

Benedetta Lanfranchi

Indiana University Press

This book is a publication of

Indiana University Press
Office of Scholarly Publishing
Herman B Wells Library 350
1320 East 10th Street
Bloomington, Indiana 47405 USA

iupress.org

First Printing 2025

Cataloging information is available from the Library of Congress.

ISBN 978-0-253-07398-3 (hdbk.)
ISBN 978-0-253-07399-0 (pbk.)
ISBN 978-0-253-07401-0 (ebook)
ISBN 978-0-253-07400-3 (web PDF)

*I dedicate this book
to my great philosophy teacher
and life mentor,
Professor D. A. Masolo*

Contents

Acknowledgments

THERE ARE MANY people who have contributed to this book and whom I want to thank. First of all, my PhD supervisor at SOAS, Professor Alena Rettová, who agreed to take me and my research project on in 2011 and who patiently and attentively guided me through the PhD process—together with my other two wonderful PhD supervisors, Phil Clark and Lindiwe Dovey—until its successful completion. The ideas in this book took shape in the course of endless chats in Alena's SOAS office with our mugs of "mud" coffee.

I want to thank all the people in Uganda who sat with me, sometimes for hours, discussing the content of this book, sharing their knowledge, wisdom, traditions, and thoughts with me; their voices literally make this book. Special thanks go to: Father Okumu, who also gave me a beautiful place to stay and delicious food every time I was in Gulu, and who dedicated so much quality time to answer my endless questions; Professor Mukasa Luutu, for inviting me to the vibrant Marcus Garvey Pan Afrikan Institute in Mbale, an experience that I will cherish forever and for which I am truly honored; Ron Atkinson and Wilfred Lajul, for sharing their wellspring of knowledge on Acholi history, culture and philosophy.

I want to thank Professor Mahmood Mamdani and the MISR community in Kampala, whose critical feedback on my research was invaluable.

I want to thank Chris Dolan, Lyandro Komakech, and Stephen Oola for taking me into the RLP Research Team while I was doing fieldwork in Uganda; their profound knowledge and acute analysis of the sociopolitical context—which they so generously and passionately shared with me—together with their informed and humane activism have had a profound influence on this book.

I want to thank Holly Porter for her generosity and hospitality in Gulu, and for really delving into the philosophical analysis of key Acholi concepts with me.

I want to thank Adam Branch for his scholarship, which was so important in the formulation of my own thoughts and analysis, and for the many great conversations in Kampala, Gulu, and over the phone.

I want to thank Professor Cosimo Zene from SOAS for giving me Gramsci, for helping me frame the methodology of this book when I was at a loss and for always encouraging me to stay true to myself intellectually and ethically.

I want to thank Professor Kai Kresse for examining my PhD thesis and pushing it to publication level with his comments and suggestions, and also for involving me in the Rethinking Sage Philosophy project, which is what really helped me make sense of my fieldwork experience in northern Uganda.

I want to thank Professor Masolo for his infinite guidance in seeing this manuscript through as well as the dream team at IUP—from Dee Mortensen to Anna Francis to Bethany Mowry to David Miller to Allison Gudenau—who have skillfully guided me in my first publication project.

I want to thank my dear friend Laetitia Bader for helping me come up with the title and for always offering an attentive listening ear and insightful feedback.

And last but certainly not least, I want to thank my family: my beloved husband, Matteo, for without his constant intellectual, emotional, and material support this book would not have seen the light. My mother, Luisa, for sacrificing many outings with her girlfriends to read through 101 drafts of the manuscript and for always having something brilliant to add. My father, Edoardo, for entertaining endless conversations with me on my PhD topic and for raising me to believe that justice and love are the most important things in life. My sister, Martina, for her incessant radical prodding whenever I risk falling into apolitical centrism—a prodding that in many ways has kept the desire for this book going.

And finally, my children, Nina and Sami, for curiously, patiently, and excitingly experiencing with me the production of my first book.

List of Acronyms

ARLPI	Acholi Religious Leaders Peace Initiative
ATJMs	Acholi Traditional Justice Mechanisms
CAR	Central African Republic
CBO	Community-Based Organization
CODESA	Convention for a Democratic South Africa
CPA	Comprehensive Peace Agreement
CSO	Civil Society Organization
CoH	Cessation of Hostilities
DDR	Disarmament, Demobilization, and Reintegration
DP	Democratic Party
DPP	Director of Public Prosecutions
DRC	Democratic Republic of the Congo
FPA	Final Peace Agreement
GoU	Government of Uganda
HURIFO	Human Rights Focus
HURIPEC	Human Rights Peace Centre
HSMF	Holy Spirit Mobile Forces
IATJ	Institute for African Transitional Justice
ICC	International Criminal Court
ICD	International Crimes Division
IDP/s	Internally Displaced Person/s
JLOS	Justice Law and Order Sector
KKA	Ker Kwaro Acholi
KY	Kabaka Yekka
LC/s	Local Council/s
LRA	Lord's Resistance Army

NGO	Nongovernmental organization/s
NRA	National Resistance Army
NRM	National Resistance Movement
NTJP	National Transitional Justice Policy
NUPI	Northern Uganda Peace Initiative
RC/s	Resistance Council/s
TJMs	Traditional Justice Mechanisms
TRC	Truth and Reconciliation Commission
ULRC	Uganda Law Reform Commission
UNC	Uganda National Congress
UNLA	Ugandan National Liberation Army
UNLM	Ugandan National Liberation Movement
UPC	Uganda Peoples' Congress
UPDA	Uganda Peoples' Democratic Army
UPDLA	Uganda People's Democratic Liberation Army
UPDF	Uganda People's Defence Forces
USAID	United States Aid for International Development

PHILOSOPHIES OF JUSTICE IN ACHOLI

Introduction

In MARCH 2009 I moved from Rome to Kampala, where I worked for a local human rights NGO on political space rights in the lead-up to the 2011 presidential election. It was a time of delicate political transitions in Uganda; this was only the second multiparty election to be held in the country since the National Resistance Movement (NRM) led by Yoweri Kaguta Museveni had come to power in 1986 and the twenty-year civil war between the government and the Lord's Resistance Army (LRA)—a guerrilla group led by Joseph Kony and made up mostly of abductees—had finally come to an end with the Juba peace talks (2006–08) and the signing of agreed-on agenda items.[1]

The war had ravaged areas of eastern and northwestern Uganda as well as areas of South Sudan, the Democratic Republic of the Congo (DRC), and the Central African Republic (CAR), but the most affected area of all was Acholi (or Acholiland) in northern Uganda, a region where it is estimated that the LRA abducted about sixty-six thousand people (UNOHCHR 2011)—of which at least thirty thousand were children and youths (Baines 2007)—and where at least one million (amounting to 90 to 95 percent of the Acholi population) were internally displaced and confined to Internally Displaced Person (IDP) camps by the Uganda People's Defense Forces (UPDF), where tens of thousands perished from disease and violence.[2]

While the total number of casualties caused by the conflict remains uncalculated, the number of adults and children who were subjected to killing; torture; or cruel, inhumane, or degrading treatment, abduction, slavery, forced marriage, forced recruitment, mutilation, sexual violence, serious psychological harm, or forced displacement was estimated to be in the tens of thousands (UNOHCHR 2011), creating a scenario whereby at the end of the war "virtually no one in Acholi remain[ed] untouched by the violence" (Atkinson 2010a, 283).

Though the LRA had formed in Acholiland as an antigovernment guerrilla group meant to defend Acholi political and economic interests, its greatest victims ended up being Acholi civilians, who were also systematically victimized by the government forces fighting the LRA. In fact, the entire Acholi population was collectively victimized by the two sides for twenty long years—by LRA leader Joseph Kony for not supporting the LRA enough and by the Government of Uganda (GoU) and the UPDF for being potential LRA rebels or supporters.[3]

The scale of the atrocities that had been committed in the context of the prolonged conflict rendered the question of justice a politically urgent one. Uganda was the first case ever to be investigated by the newly created International Criminal Court (ICC), following state referral in December 2003, on the basis of which arrest warrants were issued for five top LRA commanders on counts of crimes against humanity and war crimes.[4] Despite the Ugandan government's appeal to the ICC to deal with what it framed as an unprecedented situation of crimes against humanity, Agenda Item Three of the Juba peace talks—the Agreement on Accountability and Reconciliation (2007)—clearly maintains that the occurrence of these "new crimes" in Ugandan history do not defy the applicability of its traditional justice mechanisms: "Uganda has institutions and mechanisms, customs and usages . . . capable of addressing the crimes and human rights violations committed during the conflict" (Agreement on Accountability and Reconciliation 2007, 6).

The Agreement on Accountability and Reconciliation (together with its annexure) came to provide the legal framework for the drafting of a National Transitional Justice Policy (NTJP) by the Justice Law and Order Sector (JLOS).[5] The agreement formally introduced the use of traditional justice mechanisms within the Ugandan judiciary, mentioning the justice processes of those Ugandan communities that were most affected by the war, which included Culo Kwor and Mato Oput from the Acholi and Kayo Kuc, Ailuc, and Tonu Ci Koka from the Iteso, Langi, and Madi communities.

By providing an alternative to criminal law, this agenda item of the Juba peace talks in particular opened up a terrain for debate on which tradition of jurisprudence the country would draw on and rely on in its pursuit of justice. For over twenty years, the government had been employing different approaches to try to put a definitive end to the conflict, ranging from military operations (such as Operation North in 1991, Iron Fist Offensive in 2002, Iron Fist Offensive II in 2004, and Operation Lighting Thunder in 2008); to blanket amnesty (through the promulgation of the Amnesty Act in 2000); to peace talks (starting from state minister for the pacification of northern Uganda Betty Bigombe's efforts to engage the LRA in talks in 1994 up to the Juba peace talks). These had been coupled with a scattering of judicial mandates across a wide array of institutions and institutional figures tasked with delivering some form of justice for the many victims of the war, ranging from pardon to criminal justice to transitional justice to traditional justice and from national courts to traditional chiefs and spiritual leaders to the ICC. The heterogeneity of the jurisprudential response in dealing with the northern Ugandan war is indicative of the complexity of the justice question in the context of this conflict. This complexity was manifest not only at the level of the institutions tasked with the judgment of crimes against humanity that had been committed in Uganda but also at the theoretical level reflected in heated public debates concerning which legal canon and which tradition of jurisprudence Uganda should draw on—Western, international, criminal, civil, African, indigenous, traditional, formal, informal—in dealing with the moral and material legacies of the conflict.

As a fresh philosophy graduate from La Sapienza University, having just defended my MA thesis on Hannah Arendt's theory of judgment, I could not avoid feeling intensely drawn to debates that were raising fundamental questions regarding the very essence of an idea and practice that has been at the heart of philosophical inquiry from antiquity to the present day because of its centrality in human affairs: justice.

What captured my attention so profoundly at the time were the advocacy efforts by many Acholi (and also non-Acholi) scholars, intellectuals, activists, and spiritual leaders to include Acholi traditional justice mechanisms as the most appropriate jurisprudence for dealing with the legacy of the war. The last of the IDP camps were being dismantled, and Acholi society faced the immense challenge of reconstituting itself with perpetrators returning to live side by side with their victims, the majority of whom had been forcibly conscripted by the LRA, at least half of whom as children.[6]

My interest in understanding what was different and unique in the Acholi approach to justice is what led me to pursue a PhD in African philosophy at the School of Oriental and African Studies (SOAS) in London, which I began in 2011, at a time when the events I talk about were temporally near, urging me to write about them in the present tense in my dissertation. As I now complete the book, more than ten years have passed since the start of my research. This temporal gap, as well as my physical distance from Uganda, where I last lived in 2017–19, compels me to now write about the subject matter in the past tense.

Philosophies of Justice in Acholi: Responsibility in Times of Collective Suffering argues that Acholi Traditional Justice Mechanisms (ATJMs) were so strongly advocated for in the aftermath of the war because they provide measures to address the collective and social dimensions of responsibility that characterize theaters of wide-scale harm and suffering, which the criminal justice system neither aims for nor endeavors to address. While the limits of criminal justice in addressing the legacies of mass atrocities have been thoroughly explored, especially in the field of transitional justice, the debate within transitional justice circles has too often been framed in terms of "the peace versus justice debate."[7] By restricting the notion of justice to its legal dimension, this debate has actually managed to ignore the conceptual drama underlying it, which is that it is the very *idea* of justice that is under debate. *Philosophies of Justice* maintains that this is not only a practical but also a philosophical question and must be approached as such. A philosophical approach to the postwar Ugandan justice debate enables moving beyond the peace versus justice dichotomy and acknowledging the existence of ideas of justice for which peace is an inherent aspect rather than an alternative.

The philosophical perspective is one that is generally missing from the abundant humanitarian and academic literature on the northern Ugandan war, which thoroughly covers the psychological, religious, sociological, anthropological, political, and legal dimensions of the conflict and its aftermath.[8] Instead, the analysis conducted in these pages is prevalently theoretical and is aimed at engaging with the *ideas* of justice that are at the heart of ATJMs. The philosophical interpretation of ideas of justice is conducted mainly by analyzing the manner in which responsibility for wrongdoing is framed in Acholi traditions of moral thought and jurisprudence. This is a profoundly different type of endeavor to that of providing a balanced account of the many different sentiments and priorities regarding justice processes among afflicted community members, many of whom would undoubtedly not choose ATJMs as their preferred justice mechanism and would instead favor criminal prosecutions. This book, however, does not aim to engage in debates concerning the Acholi population's preference of one justice system over another or in debates concerning which justice response is more fair and appropriate to respond to the mass violence committed in Acholiland. Drawing on in-depth accounts of ATJMs that I gathered in the course of extended dialogues in Acholiland between 2012 and 2014, in this book I focus on philosophies of justice that belong to the Acholi tradition.

Throughout the book I refer to my fieldwork sources as dialogues rather than interviews, since the intention of this research was never to uncover "the Acholi worldview" by trying to make myself transparent and neutral before local informants who would carry on as undisturbed by me as possible; rather, the intention was to engage in philosophical conversations where both myself and the persons I dialogued with were openly invested in the quest for justice as a fundamentally human quest that concerns us all, though articulated in different languages and cultural traditions. My investment and involvement in this quest necessarily imply that the Acholi philosophies of justice described here are the fruit of my own readings and interpretations, and never at any point in this book do I presume to be depicting or capturing an "Acholi philosophy" in its entirety, a task that I believe is not only epistemologically unviable but also ethically and politically undesirable.

Philosophies of Justice in Acholi is interested in presenting ATJMs as valuable world philosophical resources, not only for the Acholi people as they struggle to reconstruct the social fabric of their community in the aftermath of the war but for human beings everywhere seeking justice. While the book seeks to showcase the cultural and linguistic rootedness of Acholi traditional jurisprudences, it also aims to engage the philosophical universality of Acholi ideas of justice, arguing that these ideas can be understood and applied across the world in humanity's global struggle for justice. By presenting Acholi jurisprudence as culturally particular and unique but not insular, the book insists on cultural particularity *and* universality—to echo Ghanaian philosopher Kwasi Wiredu (1996)—when approaching ideas of justice in the Acholi tradition, which is why the critical engagement with ATJMs is conducted through a wide variety of sources, from Acholi to other African to Western philosophical traditions.[9]

The analytical work conducted in these pages on Acholi philosophies of justice is in no way upheld *against* ideas of justice contained in international or domestic criminal law. What are presented here are important contributions from Acholi as well as other African jurisprudences on what constitutes justice, but these are never antagonistically endorsed as substitutes for criminal justice or individually sanctioned human rights, when and if these are in fact protected by national and international institutions. The aim of this book is not to speak *against* these levels of justice but rather to speak to *other* levels of justice: those that address the collective dimension of suffering that follows injustices committed on a large scale.

The complexity of researching Acholi philosophies of justice is presented in chapter 1, where I discuss the epistemological and ethical challenges involved in researching oral and communal philosophies in an unknown language. In this chapter I present my idea of philosophical fieldwork as the main research methodology for this project. I devised this method through a comparative reading of two twentieth-century thinkers' intellectual projects: Kenyan philosopher Henry Odera Oruka's sage philosophy and Italian political activist and intellectual Antonio Gramsci's philosophy of praxis. Both thinkers divide philosophy into two orders: the first order entails a dimension of philosophy that is not strictly academic or scholarly and that lives instead in popular culture and expression while the second order entails a critical self-reflective activity. For both thinkers, only in the continuous and mutual tapping into one another of first- and second-order philosophy can philosophy be that life force aimed at resolving human problems and carry emancipatory potential. In *Philosophies of Justice in Acholi*, philosophical fieldwork features as the methodological tool for accessing first order philosophy and for putting it in conversation with second-order philosophy.

To situate the study of Acholi ideas of justice in historical and geographical contexts, in chapter 2 I provide a brief background of the events leading up to and characterizing the northern Uganda war. This chapter contains a detailed description—derived from secondary literature and from my own interviews—of the many steps entailed in the Acholi traditional justice process. It also contextualizes the institutional provision for ATJMs in Uganda's current judiciary.

In chapter 3 I analyze the concept of community-based collective responsibility that informs ATJMs by focusing on the three Acholi beings *jok* (god or spirit), *abila* (ancestral shrine), and *cen* (vengeance ghost) and by analyzing them in terms of different attributions of responsibility for wrongs committed.[10] I argue that the complex and different attributions of responsibility that each of these beings entails are key to understanding the overall meaning and aim of ATJMs. I show that by framing responsibility in terms of jok, abila, and cen, a justice process that looks at the deep and far-reaching causes for widespread suffering is enabled. This process is based on a conception of moral personhood constituted beyond the individual sphere, and that includes a series of other beings—material and non, living and non, human and non—that all have a bearing on individuals' and groups' lives and actions. I discuss these Acholi moral philosophies in relation to theories of punishment and theories of personhood in African philosophy.

In chapter 4, the final chapter, I first engage with the two most important critiques that have been raised against the use of ATJMs in the aftermath of the northern Ugandan war: collective guilt and ethnojustice. I then question the extent to which the contemporary mobilizations of ATJMs in the aftermath of the war can be analyzed in a framework of what Mahmood Mamdani (2014; 2015; 2020) terms "political justice," which refers to a justice processes that is inclusive, affecting groups, and aimed at political reform.

My general conclusion is that by centering collectivity in justice processes and by framing both the causes and the effects of mass violence as prerogatives of a justice process, ATJMs integrally carry a political understanding of justice. The ability of ATJMs to frame responsibility in terms of community-based collective responsibility produces a holistic notion of wrong where the focus is not strictly on individual culpability but rather on the wider environment within which individual wrongdoers operate and within which individual acts of violence are perpetuated.

This holistic notion of responsibility provides a profound understanding of the nature of mass violence as a type of violence that is committed against a collectivity—a group, a community, a people—that is not to be intended as a sum of individual lives but as *a collective life*. ATJMs frame responsibility in a way that maintains individuals and groups in relation and not as separate entities while not conflating collective responsibility with collective guilt. While the line that separates collective responsibility and collective guilt may appear to be a fine one, the book clearly differentiates the community-based collective responsibility principle contained in ATJMs from processes of collective guilt by focusing on its truth-seeking dimension, which is aimed at taking on collective suffering without remaining trapped in it. While collective guilt may lead to a sense of shame and taboo over one's history, collective responsibility instead *may* become a way for communities that have been affected by mass violence to morally, socially, and politically reconstitute themselves by gaining agency over their histories of violence.

However, the book also concludes that while ATJMs are both conceptually and historically oriented toward political justice, their application in the context following the northern Ugandan war so far falls short of political justice proper because they have not yet been able to address the full picture of responsibility of *all* parties to the conflict, focusing instead almost exclusively on the responsibilities of the Acholi.

The northern Ugandan war was in fact two wars in one: an intra-Acholi civil conflict between LRA supporters and Acholi civilians and a civil war between the LRA and the government. The way ATJMs have been thought of and the way in which they engaged in postwar Acholi intellectual culture have focused mainly—if not exclusively—on the intra-Acholi dimension of the conflict. While this can be seen as a political resolution to the first level of the conflict—because it reconstitutes a strong relationality between individual Acholi perpetrators and survivors and the larger Acholi polity—it leaves the second level of the conflict, that between Acholiland and the Ugandan state, largely unaddressed. Without addressing this level of the conflict, a proper political justice process cannot be achieved.

I do not believe, as many critics would, that this gap is due to limitations of the ATJMs themselves. My contention throughout this book is that the jurisprudential foundations of ATJMs make them applicable beyond the confines of the traditional Acholi polity within which they originate, though this necessarily would involve adaptation and changes to some aspects of the traditional process regarding, for example, which human and nonhuman beings are involved. Rather, I believe that the gap in the Acholi and Uganda political justice process is due to the absence of a national platform on which to reconcile the Acholi and government/state parties to the conflict. The length of time it has taken to develop the NTJP—which was completed only in 2019 and which is still waiting to be transcribed into law—is hindering this wider process of political justice at the national level.

The NTJP currently includes truth telling and reparations as key pieces of national building and reconciliation (Republic of Uganda 2019).

Both aspects have at their heart the question of responsibility, with truth telling providing a platform for framing responsibility and reparations providing a platform for accountability. I believe that the way these will be provided for under national law, and the space that will be given to the ideas of justice carried in ATJMs, will determine the extent and the nature of Uganda's political justice process, which is still in the making.

1   Methodological Considerations

THIS RESEARCH DRAWS on three levels of philosophy: Indigenous Acholi knowledge systems; African philosophical frameworks that inform the communal character of the definition and practice of justice among the Acholi people of northern Uganda; and a comparative reading of the major moral and legal questions arising in the Acholi context with select Western philosophers and select debates in Western moral thought and jurisprudence.

My sources for analysis are both oral and written. The oral sources consist of twenty-two long, in-depth oral dialogues (recorded between 2012 and 2014) with selected interlocutors that include academics, philosophers, clan leaders, political leaders, elders, lawyers, justice sector representatives, nongovernmental organization (NGO) workers, members of civil society, religious leaders, and community opinion leaders. Excerpts from dialogues with these interlocutors are quoted throughout the book. Where written consent was obtained, full names and titles are provided; where it was not possible to obtain consent for the transcription of the interviews, pseudonyms or generic identifiers such as *youth* and *elder* have been used. Other oral sources are key discussions I personally witnessed and participated in, such as during the course of the ICC Review Conference in 2010, which I attended as a member of the Italian delegation; during consultations on the national transitional justice policy draft among the third Institute for African Transitional Justice (IATJ), the Justice Law and Order Sector (JLOS), and civil society, which I attended in 2013 as a researcher with the Refugee Law Project (RLP); and in the course of seminars that I attended at the philosophy department of Makerere University. My written sources consist of secondary academic, humanitarian, and advocacy literature on ATJMs.

The majority of the interlocutors in this book are Acholi. Despite the differences that characterize them, all of the Acholi interlocutors who feature in this book were strongly involved in activist work with affected communities, and their reliance on Acholi traditional practices was strongly influenced by their perceptions of community members' needs and requests in the aftermath of the war. Many of them turned to ATJMs in an effort to provide guidance, solace, or accountability to community members who were suffering trauma, poverty, and illness as a result of twenty years of conflict.

Tradition and Philosophy

In Acholi, *traditional* is used to refer to one of the many bodies of knowledge that constitute present-day Acholi cultural, sociopolitical, religious, economic, and philosophical life. Lajul maintains that *traditional* is the most accurate translation for what in Acholi would be described as *kwo kwaro* or *kwo macon*. The word *kwaro* in Acholi means *ancestors*, so these two terms literally translate as "the life of the ancestors" and "the way Acholi people lived their lives." According to Lajul, *kwaro* is most commonly used to refer to the historical dimension of Acholi customs, philosophies, religions, and institutions. This term is also used to signify Indigenous, and one can often hear people in Acholi referring to *ngec kwaro* (Indigenous knowledge), *cam kwaro* (Indigenous food), *myel kwaro* (Indigenous or traditional dance), and *wer kwaro* (Indigenous songs).[1] This choice of terminology is also in line with that of Harlacher et al. (2006, 9) in their use of *traditions* and *traditional* to mean "what the local people who have been interviewed consider them to mean": "Traditional . . . means essentially the living traditions of the people—living in memory and imagination, living in interpretations of the world, and living in the practices of the Acholi people in contemporary Northern Central Uganda."

The Acholi terms and phrases used to speak of traditions that Harlacher et al. (2006, 9) found in their study were *cik Acholi* (the law of Acholi), *tic Acholi* (Acholi rituals and procedures), *kit ma Acholi macon gitimo* (the way Acholi did it in the old days), and *kit ma Acholi macon giniang* (the way Acholi understood or interpreted it in the old days). Finally, as emphasized by the Acholi philosopher Daniel Komakech, the use of the term *traditional* is in line with a hermeneutic approach that links the past with the future: "Meaning, and thus knowledge, is therefore an interpretation that is always situated within a living tradition and our inescapable historicity, which is a particular 'horizon' of understanding based on culture and personal presuppositions. . . . Accordingly, hermeneutics takes the full measure of our historical and cultural embeddedness" (Komakech 2012, 132).

Philosophical hermeneutics assigns a prominent role to history and culture in the interpretation of philosophical concepts (Heidegger [1927] 2008; Gadamer [1960] 2013). This book's focus on tradition is not aimed at imposing past ways of life, nor at undermining contemporary Acholi and Ugandan realities that are also informed in important ways by the experience of colonization and globalization, but simply at understanding Acholi justice mechanisms as constituting a specific tradition of thought and practice—in terms of both content and style—that can be hermeneutically interpreted within a historical horizon of references. The fact that these are specific orientations in thought rather than reflections of unanimous collective worldviews is attested to by the profound variety of interpretations that the different interlocutors of this project incline toward in their own presentations of ATJMs and the concepts of justice therein enshrined. However, this book's positioning toward distinctive ideas by individuals or groups is to read them as specific *orientations in thought* rather than as single, individual expressions. This means that this book's focus is always on tradition as a *shared body of thought endowed with historical life*.

The book's focus on tradition should not be misread as a glorification of all tradition. This book in fact discriminates between tradition's positive and negative potentials and identifies as positive only that use of tradition that helps articulate emancipatory goals and achieve emancipatory ends for as many community members as possible. This is much in line with the Beninese philosopher Paulin Hountondji's notion of "endogenous" (1995; 1997), which has largely informed the intellectual debate concerning the African continent's philosophical identity from the 1960s to the 1990s. According to Hountondji, African philosophy had a huge role to play in repairing the painful alienation that resulted from Africa's colonization. African philosophy could assist in the recuperation of the Continent's Indigenous knowledges and knowledge base in an effort to counter its economic, political, and cultural dependence on the former colonizing powers, which was by definition extroverted. Hountondji actually favors the concept of endogenous knowledge to both Indigenous and traditional knowledge because, in his opinion, it allows one "to dwell on the origin of a cultural product or value that comes from, or at least is perceived by people as coming from inside their own society, as opposed to imported or 'exogenous' products or values—though we should admit, in a sense, that there is no absolute origin at all, and the concept of endogeneity itself should therefore be relativized" (Hountondji 1995, 6–7).

The definition of Indigenous—or, better yet, endogenous—that I take from the African philosophy debate is thus not strictly cultural-ist or traditionalist in a sense that could incur essentialization or rei-fication. For the African philosophers who were seriously invested in the debate, such as Paulin Hountondji, D. A. Masolo, Kwasi Wiredu, Kwame Gyekye, Peter Bodunrin, and Odera Oruka, indigeneity was not to be wielded as a trophy against the colonial powers, for this would end up glorifying all Indigenous and traditional knowledges, even those that were not useful for Africa's economic development and political freedom. Hountondji, for one, always attributed a great risk to an "un-considered imposition of the word 'philosophy'" (1989, 8) on African traditions of thought that would end up giving them "a unanimistic and idealistic interpretation, by emptying them of their real dynamism and complexity, by isolating them from the economic, social and political context which gives them meaning" (9).

For all of these reasons, this book's narrative never stops at the level of description of Acholi traditions and critically engages with every con-cept, idea, and belief encountered in the course of fieldwork through a specific research methodology that I call philosophical fieldwork.

Philosophical Fieldwork

My method of philosophical fieldwork draws importantly on Kenyan philosopher Odera Oruka's sage philosophy method. Oruka undertook his sage philosophy project soon after being hired by the University of Nairobi's philosophy department in the early 1970s (Presbey 2023). The project aimed at collecting "the sagacious and philosophical thinking of indigenous Africans whose lives are rooted in the cultural milieu of traditional Africa" (Oruka 1991a, 1). Oruka wanted to expand philoso-phy's reach beyond Eurocentric canons in his own Kenyan context to help rectify the legacy of destruction and/or subordination of endog-enous knowledge systems perpetuated by colonialism that contrib-uted to keeping Africans in a condition of material and spiritual un-derdevelopment. His sage philosophy approach meant to open a third way for African philosophy, one that could elude the trap of ethnophilosophy without collapsing entirely into professional philosophy, the two main camps within which African philosophy was oriented from the late 1970s.

Hountondji had denounced ethnophilosophy as a second-rate philosophical discourse reserved for Africa, spearheaded by Belgian missionary Placide Tempels in his *Bantu Philosophy* ([1945] 1959), which turned collective myths, folklore, and cultural practices into an anonymously and unconsciously held worldview of "the Bantus" (Hountondji [1976] 1983). Meanwhile, professional philosophy was criticized at the time for accepting the established standards of Western academia at the risk of alienating much African intellectual production that did not fit into these standards. Oruka thus presented sage philosophy as a third alternative between ethnophilosophy and professional philosophy (Kresse and Nyarwath 2023).

The project of revisiting sage philosophy has recently been the subject of an edited publication on Oruka titled *Rethinking Sage Philosophy: Interdisciplinary Perspective on and Beyond Henry Odera Oruka* (2023), which explores the ways in which it is worthwhile to reengage with Oruka today. Though this publication postdates my fieldwork, the ideas and reflections that inform it were very much at the heart of my own research approach, so I feel I can refer to them as informing my methodology. I would have benefited greatly at the time from the clarity with which the book explicates the aspects of sage philosophy that, in the editors' opinion, remain relevant and important and those that need to be improved for future research.

In terms of my own research project, one aspect of Oruka's sage philosophy project that was not relevant, for example, was the search for "uncontaminated" African intellectual resources. Oruka's research was moved largely by the desire to search for African intellectual content that was independent of Western culture. For my own research, I felt that not only was uncontamination no longer a realistic possibility in the year 2012, when I began to record my dialogues (more than twenty to forty years after Oruka interviewed the Kenyan sages), but it was also not conducive to the type of philosophical investigation I wanted to carry out. Almost all of my interlocutors were not only fluent English speakers but also highly conversant with traditions of Western moral and legal thought because of having undergone formal education (and, in some cases, legal training) and were close—if not devoted—to the Christian faith. Formal education, Christianity, and the English language have so profoundly impacted Acholi society and culture that it appeared to me not only paradoxical but also unhelpful to try to demarcate a terrain of indigeneity separate from these influences.

Diverse cultural, religious, and philosophical traditions are intimately blended together in present-day Acholi, drawing and feeding on each other constantly, as evidenced in all of my dialogues where people refer to their ancestors as sources of moral guidance with the same ease and immediacy with which they quote the Bible. As I was particularly interested in understanding contemporary discussions and debates around justice, it did not make sense for me to seek out interlocutors who were knowledgeable only with regard to the past but rather the opposite: I was interested in interlocutors who were rooted in Acholi contemporaneity in its multiple manifestations, languages, traditions, and beliefs.

The ways in which I blend popular oral philosophical accounts with academic philosophical literature is again profoundly informed by the Orukian understanding of philosophy as comprised of a first and second order, which I relate to the Italian intellectual Antonio Gramsci's idea of philosophy. Both thinkers divide philosophy into two orders: the first entails a dimension of philosophy that is neither strictly academic nor scholarly and lives instead in popular culture and expression; the second entails a critical, self-reflective activity. In my comparative study of the two thinkers, I argue that both Oruka and Gramsci point to the importance of empirical experience in philosophy, which is what I have called "philosophical fieldwork" (Lanfranchi 2023). Philosophical fieldwork is a key methodological tool for accessing that first order of philosophy, which Oruka and Gramsci value as a vital epistemological and moral source for the human community. Only in the first and second orders of philosophy's continuous and mutual tapping into one another can philosophy be that life force aimed at resolving human problems, as worded by Kresse in a 1995 interview with Oruka: "For Oruka it is the sage—and not the philosopher—who has at heart the 'ethical betterment of the community that he lives in'" (Graness and Kresse 1997, 254).

It is for this reason that the first and second orders of philosophy must remain in contact: to guarantee the "ethical obligation for philosophy as a whole in regard to the well-being of society and humanity at large" (Graness and Kresse 1997, 251). Underlying both thinkers' careful distinction between these two orders and the way they relate to one another is their notion of philosophy as an emancipatory endeavor, and it is this particular spirit of philosophy that I am interested in pursuing in this book.

In "Philosophy and Indigenous Knowledge: An African Perspective," Masolo writes that "indeed, a look back might now suggest that at least part of the controversy over ethnophilosophy was about how the indigenous was to be represented" (Masolo 2003 31). He then provides his own definition of the Indigenous as comprising the everyday and the familiar together with "the historical nature and character of ideas" (22).

Hountondji was critical of separating philosophical themes and content from peoples' everyday lived realities because in that way not only would philosophy not provide people with useful tools for understanding and transforming their realities but it could actually inhibit this process by making their relationships with their surrounding realities incomprehensible and unattainable. As relationships with reality take place through peoples' consciousness, "staffing Africans' consciousnesses with . . . objects that do not exist" alienates them not only from their surrounding realities but from themselves, making even their own subjective experiences unintelligible. Instead, being that the Indigenous "is the whole realm of what constitutes our consciousness" (Masolo 2003, 31), it must remain at the center of philosophical reflection, constituting a philosophical resource to be critically examined.

The crucial aspect of the Indigenous/academic dialectic as exposed by Masolo and Hountondji (but also Gramsci and Oruka) is that conducting philosophy in isolation or removal from its lived context is precisely what eliminates its emancipatory potential. That is why the method I use in this book entails conducting extensive philosophical conversations with knowledgeable members of the community, recording them, and putting that first level of philosophy in contact with second-level philosophy through critical analysis by way of academic philosophy and in turn by testing academic philosophy's discoveries against those in the dialogues.

The Word *Justice*—Reflections on Language

Many of the discussions and deliberations on the use of ATJMs that I witnessed in Uganda were conducted in the English language. This was partly due to their institutional provision under an internationally brokered peace agreement and national legislation involving a variety of stakeholders whose common language was English. English was thus a key language in this particular debate on justice after the war, often spearheaded by members of Acholi society who either produced academic literature on the topic in English or engaged in national or international consultations in English on the use of criminal and traditional justice.

Most of the key knowledgeable persons in Acholi whom I was pointed to by community members were fluent English speakers, with the exception of some of the elders and rwots, whom I talked to with the assistance of an interpreter. While some of the interlocutors were not completely fluent in English, most had enough knowledge of the language to enable direct and high-quality communication without the need of an interpreter.

That said, it is undeniable that many of the interesting debates at the time were obviously taking place in the Acholi language, and those I have unfortunately not been able to analyze due to my ignorance of Acholi Luo, which I was simply not able to learn in the time span of my PhD, mainly due to the difficulty in finding a Luo teacher in London. So while I was fortunately able to engage in very meaningful and rich discussions in English, I cannot deny that I have been precluded from debate on philosophies of justice in Acholi due to my inability to speak Luo. One way I tried to compensate for this shortcoming was by putting my ignorance to conceptual use by playing with—and even forcing—literal translations of key terms. One of my recurrent questions, for example, asked for the Acholi literal translation of the English word *justice*. This question was always followed by a long silence and then a long discussion that signaled it was not a matter of mere linguistic translation but entailed a profound conceptual dimension:

> Justice in Acholi? That is a challenge now. . . . The word *justice* . . . I think that it is a process that is believed to happen naturally. Justice. . . . I am tempted to call it *culo kwor* but then again that is reparation. Okay, I am going to seek help on this one. [After a long pause] You see, you don't talk of justice; you talk in terms of repairing the damage. You say, "This is not a court, but it is to repair the relationships." It's the repairing of relationships; once that is repaired then that is the justice. There is no court because you don't want to already prejudge that there is wrong. You will

hear the stories of both sides, and then you will see how to bridge that relationship again. You don't apportion blame. And the chairman says it in the beginning: "This is not a court. We are not going to say right and wrong." But you are given [the opportunity] to tell your story, you are even cross-examined to find: really what is the cause? That is the reason for all that. Once that is done, we come to a middle ground. That is really why I am finding it difficult to find the word *justice* in Acholi.[2]

In the dialogue excerpt quoted above, Oola clearly posits the Acholi focus on restoration as something different from justice in the English sense, which he associates with the court system and with the apportionment of blame by a judge. He thus posits the Acholi precept of restoration and repairing relationships after conflict in opposition to a legalistic notion that he identifies with the English term for justice.

Acholi terms used to talk about justice are often highly metaphorical and need to be further explained and interpreted for meaning because, in the words of an Acholi youth, "Our words are in the form of symbols."[3] Furthermore, this attempt at literal translation proved fallacious in another way, as the linguistic challenge goes hand in hand with the strictly philosophical challenge presented by the formulation of moral questions from within the Western philosophical tradition, which I noticed were often perceived as not directly pertinent to the aims and procedures of Acholi justice practices, as an Acholi elder clearly expressed: "The only difficulty is with answering questions which are Western-oriented. The problem is that there seems to be quests for the exact thing in the African perspective, where it would not be there. It would not even be there, so the words in Acholi would not be there to describe it."[4]

Others' search for the Acholi word for justice resulted in a more conciliatory outlook between English and Acholi concepts of justice, not necessarily reflected in terminology but rather in content:

Justice is also a modern term, it's a modern invention but it's a term that is understood, even locally. . . . All those processes were justice processes because they led to accountability for a wrong that had been committed. So you would not find the word *justice* used, you would rather find those words like *mato oput* or *cullo kwor*—you know all those words. And maybe those words in themselves are justice. Because *cullo kwor* is justice and *mato oput* is also justice for someone. So you would not find justice being used as one word, but rather you would find components of justice.[5]

A similar point was reiterated by a prominent human rights lawyer: "There is no single word [for] justice because I don't think the word exists in the vocabulary of the Acholi people, but you have circumstances that if put together would amount to a Western concept of justice: these things about compensation, reparation . . . all these things put together."[6]

When I asked another legal expert from the ministry's transitional justice working group whether there is a modern Acholi word for justice, after much thought and deliberation she concluded that "justice is *ngol matir*—it is like . . . it's like taking the right decision. Yeah. *Ngol* is like a decision. Taking the right decision. That is justice."[7]

The most common translation of the Acholi word *ngol* is "to cut," though in the first Acholi dictionary by Father Crazzolara he gives three definitions of *ngol* as "to cut," "to pass a sentence," and "to decide a question" (Crazzolara 1938). In this sense, the notion of cutting comes into the question of justice, implicating fair judgment, as also explained by Porter (2013).

This sense of "cutting straight" as fair judgment was explained to me by two knowledgeable elders in their elaborations on the Acholi terms *ngol ma tir* and *ngol ma opore* as "passing judgment appropriately": "If you want to bring in the concept of judgment in its accommodative mode, then you can say *ngol ma opore* or *ngol ma atir*—that means it is based on the truth that has been uttered from both parties and then you say: 'This is the middle line we must take.'"[8]

Though most people used *ngol ma opore* as the Acholi translation of justice, the more I asked the more it emerged that this term is actually just an Acholi linguistic translation of a *Western* concept of justice, but it is not a term that reflects the Acholi sense of justice: "If you directly translate that [*ngol ma opore*] back to English that is 'proper judgment'! But that's not the Acholi thing. *Ngol ma opore* is what they use on the radio always. . . . Again, they are translating from the English, trying to make it fit."[9] A similar point is also made by Ochieng:

> *Ngol ma opore.* That is translation. You know *ngol* means judgment. But for us we don't have *ngol.* You know what we say is *mato oput*, that is reconciliation. So, what it means here in Luo is that justice is reconciliation. That you reconcile with one another. . . . You know when you talk of judgment those are two different concepts because we don't have the word *judgment*. We don't! What we have is reconciliation,

mato oput. It is not judgment. You are not judging anybody. The truth has already been established. You see what you need to see here is that I have done something wrong. I am the one who is saying I've done it. And the victim is the one who is saying: "Get back in the life, I have forgiven you." That is how you can understand what we mean.[10]

I also came across some isolated translations of justice as *riyo tal, laro lok*, and *chopo lok*. Given the conceptual complexity entailed in translating the word *justice*, I consulted the Kenyan philosopher D. A. Masolo, who is a native Luo speaker and who, together with Professor Odoch Pido from the University of Kenya, enriched the etymological and conceptual analysis by providing me with detailed written feedback. Professor Pido provided the following translations and interpretations of all the terms I gathered during my research that are used to refer to justice:

> *Ng'ol*. This works well as *ng'olo lok*, which literally means "to stop speaking"; where to speak means to generate conflict and where *lok* is conflict itself. When elders converge in a meeting to settle disputes, the main intention is to perform *ng'olo lok*, stop or resolve conflicts or feuds. *Ng'olo lok* is a pronouncement of the ruling, the direction that all must take to stop the conflict where it is or from escalating.
>
> *Ng'ol ma opore*. It is a pronouncement that is befitting of the conflict in that it brings the conflict to an end, with examples from the past and with all satisfied. Clarity, objectivity and in-step with time-seasoned experiences are important qualities of *ng'ol ma opore, ng'ol lok maber* and *ng'ol lok matir*. *Ng'olo lok labongo poro ne* (to resolve conflict without invoking past experiences) does not help because it leaves many dis-satisfied players and doing so belittles experience, knowledge and wisdom.
>
> *Ng'ol ma ber*. It is to settle disputes in ways that is proper in that it is amicable, without violence, death or loss of any kind. It also means settling disputes in a good ways; meaning, it is peaceful, happy and time enduring. *Ng'ol ma rac* is the bad ruling—*labongo tam*, without much consideration of the positive-negative consequences.
>
> *Ng'ol ma tir*. It is to settle disputes in ways that is straight, correct and right. Here to dubious, crooked, and wooly are not desirable. It also means there is a path that is correct and that to be straight is also correct or right. The characters of individuals who undertake the particular dispute should be impeccable, spotless, without doubt, upright, always impartial and able to cut the conflict in the centre.
>
> *Riyo tal*. It is an act of putting a peace stick between two warring sides. There are many types of sticks and for different purposes (*tir, oleke, odo, lut* and *tilo*) *tal* is only one of them. Acholi men used to fight

with *odoo*, a stick that would cause damage but not enough to kill. *Odoo* and *tal* are the same stick, *odoo* becomes *tal* when used to stop a fight between two men. In this case you position the stick between the two in such a way that attempts to strike one another stops at the stick—they do not hit each other. It is from this act that *riyo tal* is anything that people use to resolve conflicts.

Chopo lok. It is to end conflict, to amicably reach the end of conflict. It is similar to *tyeko lok*, finishing the conflict. A traveler is heard saying *achopo*, meaning "I have arrived" or "this is the end of the journey." From this, one can deduce that conflict resolution is similar to going on a journey, arriving at the end of a journey is like resolving a conflict.[11]

Pido thus does not identify the Acholi rendering of justice as *ngol* as necessarily implying judgment. Masolo also contributed key insights to complement Pido's detailed etymological analysis:

I do not think there is one term or word in Dholuo that translates the English word "justice." Instead, different variations of the idea *ma-chal*, or *ma-rom* (same way; equally; impartially) express what it is that requires or invokes need for just action. Here are some examples:

1. *timo ma-chal i thek*—literally "doing the same in mediation." This idea requires that when mediating in a conflict, the mediator treats the warring parties exactly the same way; that she/he be impartial in helping to end a conflict (such as a fight or a dispute over ownership of, or interest in property).

2. *pogo ma-rom* (to distribute equally). This is pretty obvious for many distributive actions, assuming that the parties involved in the claim are indeed equal in all respects. Given that the Luo are very hierarchical in different ways, this could only happen where the individuals (or the lineages they represent) are related as twins of the same gender. Hence, in most cases, everyone's just claim (*pok ng'ato*) is related to their position in the scale of seniority in the family or lineage in the clan. To claim, therefore, that justice has been done in a distributive process is to claim that the distributor knows well and has followed correctly the laid-down distributive principle that assigns everyone, or every lineage, or their representatives, their right share of the distributive good.[12]

The role of language in translating concepts across Europhone and Afrophone philosophies has been the subject of various academic positions and debates, among which is Kwasi Wiredu's (1996) famous position on the untranslatability of correspondence theory of truth into Akan, based on the fact that there is no Akan equivalent of the English words *fact* and *truth*, which are needed to formulate correspondence truth theory as "x is true if it corresponds to some fact." This led Wiredu to conclude that "the problem of the relation between truth and fact arises out of the nature of a language and, consequently, that some philosophical problems are not universal" (Graness 2019a, 32–33). Wiredu's claim against the universality of some philosophical issues, bound as they are by the languages of their expression, has been contested by Rettová (2022, 145–46), who states that "words are only arbitrarily attached to notions. . . . The mother language may restrict or shape the conceptual horizon within which we think, but it does not prevent its modification on coming into contact with another language and its conceptual articulation."

Further, as stated by Hiesmayr in her support of multilinguism for philosophy, "The recognition of one's characteristics can be facilitated by contact with foreign elements. It can expose which features are similar and which are special, and even allow some of them to be re-thought" (2022, 149–50). This means that philosophical translations can actually expand one's conceptual universe when the process of translation is envisioned as a dialogic process whereby the answers are sought together by the different parties in dialogue and not imposed by one party onto the other. Translation features in this book as a mutual endeavor, entailing self-translation and self-explication on behalf of all parties to the dialogue.

Having said all that, a prerogative of this book is that these traditional mechanisms remain inscribed within the agenda of justice and are not approached solely as healing mechanisms or as other types of cultural practices. Much of what this book actually seeks to demonstrate is that even though they may not be captured by a single and specific word that is literally translatable into the word *justice* as found in European languages, it is important to maintain the understanding of ATJMs within the conceptual and experiential domain of justice. It is in this domain that they are seen as posing a philosophical challenge to monocultural ideas and definitions of justice, and it is only from this domain that they can contribute to expanding global understandings of what justice is from a world philosophies perspective.

2   The Context

The War in Acholiland

Most scholars have traced the roots of the extreme mass violence that has characterized postcolonial Acholi back to decolonial and postcolonial Ugandan politics of the 1960s and 1970s, which exploded in the 1980–1986 Bush War.

Uganda attained independence from Britain in 1962 with a political alliance between the Kabaka Yekka (KY) party—led by Mutebi Mutesa II, the *kabaka* (king) of the southern kingdom of Buganda—and the Uganda Peoples' Congress (UPC) led by Milton Obote, a Langi from the north. This power-sharing agreement was an attempt to bridge the profound political and economic inequalities between the north and the south of the country that the British Empire had adamantly pursued during its administration of the Protectorate of Uganda (1894–1962).

Acholi was not included in the initial 1894 British Protectorate in East Africa territories, and British administration over Acholiland officially commenced with the 1899 military expedition led by Delmé-Radcliffe (Girling 1960, 151). While Atkinson (1989, 32) maintains that "the roots of Acholi ethnicity" were planted as early as 1675, he also specifies that at the time of the first written accounts by European travelers to the region in the 1860s, "the broad unity that characterized Acholi as a whole had not yet taken on any practical forms of expression" and that "neighboring groups had no occasion to deal with either the area or the people of Acholi as any sort of unit." A key factor in the shaping of Acholi identity was the arrival in the region of Arabic speakers from the north: Kutoria traders in the 1850s, followed by Jadiya representatives of the Egyptian administration of the Upper Nile in 1872. Comboni missionary priest Pasquale Crazzolara, who was stationed in northern Uganda and in Sudan for many years and wrote a history of the Luo, describes how the Kutoria gave the name Shuuli to the inhabitants of north central Uganda because their language resembled that of the Shilluk, a Luo-speaking people inhabiting what is present-day South Sudan. According to Crazzolara, the inhabitants of Acholi who were unfamiliar with the *sh* sound eventually changed the pronunciation of the Kutoria Shuuli to Cuuli and finally to Achooli (Crazzolara 1950). The appropriation of an externally given name by the inhabitants of Acholi leads Atkinson to conclude that "by the end of the nineteenth century, the people of Acholi had embraced the externally introduced Shuuli identity to the extent that they began to modify the term to fit their own needs" (Atkinson 2010a, 271).

Whereas the Arabs, Egyptians, and Europeans with whom the inhabitants of Acholi had come into contact up until the Delmé-Radcliffe expedition had diminished but not overthrown the sovereignty of the Acholi chiefs on which Acholi political and religious life was centered, with the establishment of British rule, "the tension of the interacting forces, which kept the Acholi political system in being, slackened" (Atkinson 2010a, 271).

The chiefdom was the basis of Acholi sociopolitical order, headed by a hereditary *rwot* (king, chief, or lord; plural *rwodi*) who possessed royal regalia and to whom tributes were paid (Atkinson 2010a). Each village in Acholi was named after the exogamous, patrilineal, patrilocal, and patriarchal lineage at its core, headed by the *ladit kaka* (village elder; plural *ludito* or *ladito kaka*) who was the living representative of the lineage's founder (Atkinson 2010a).[1] Traditionally, each rwot shared his authority and decision-making powers with the ludito kaka. By the time the British extended their authority over Acholi, the number of Acholi chiefdoms was 65, encompassing between 364 and 419 lineages with a total population of 125,150 inhabitants (Harlacher et al. 2006, 137).[2]

In 1900, Britain signed an agreement with the kingdom of Buganda, a highly centralized and thriving kingdom located in central Uganda under the authority of the kabaka. The agreement granted Buganda autonomy under the British Protectorate in the form of a constitutional monarchy, virtually making the Baganda "partners with the British in the advance of British imperialism in the area" (Mwanzi 1981, 162). British colonial offices were established in the northern towns of Gulu (in 1910) and Kitgum (in 1914) (Paine 2014), and Baganda officials were employed as functionaries of the colonial government in the setup of a centralized and hierarchical political structure that was easier to control than the various autonomous chiefdoms (Harlacher et al. 2006).

Resistance to early British intrusion into Acholiland culminated in the Lamogi rebellion of 1913, headed by rwot Awic of Payera, who was ultimately defeated and imprisoned in Kampala. Episodes of armed resistance informed the colonial government's selective policy on the distribution of rifles in the region, to ensure the firearms would not be turned against the government. The chiefs to whom rifles were distributed "maintained a monopoly of force, using it for self-aggrandizement and as an instrument of vengeance against old and new rivals" (Behrend 1999, 17), creating a situation in which most Acholi began to regard these chiefs as "mere tools of an oppressive and alien regime" (Karugire 1980, 150).

The new political structure the British introduced undercut one of the crucial characteristics of the Acholi precolonial polity: the limited power and authority of those at its head, which had been traditionally maintained through the rwot's sharing of political power with constituent village lineage heads; the possibility for dissatisfied members of the chiefdoms to migrate; the bar on the rwot to access arms and special fighting forces; and the ban on the rwot's monopoly over the army, whose command he had to share with the lineage heads and elders (Atkinson 2010a). This delicate balance of power changed with the colonial administration's division of Acholiland into six counties, each headed by a county chief who was also called rwot but who was not necessarily a rwot according to Acholi custom—that is, the county rwot did not belong to the chiefdom lineage and did not possess the qualities befitting a rwot such as "generosity, intelligence, good listening skills, the ability to speak persuasively and, perhaps most importantly, an excellent sense of judgement and the ability to mediate and arbitrate inter-clan conflicts within the chiefdom" (Harlacher et al. 2006, 26).[3]

Together with the profound political inequalities introduced by the colonial administration of Acholiland, disparity in the accumulation of wealth was enhanced during this period. Such disparity strongly impacted the social order, particularly at the intrahousehold level, resulting in the breaking up of groups of kin (Girling 1960). With the administration of the population as a discrete tribal unit and the emphasis on "sharply differentiated and exclusivist tribal cultures and identities" (Atkinson 2010a, 7) in a context of competition for "scarce social and economic investments and opportunities" (7), the colonial government thus contributed to the creation of an Acholi tribe. This identity was further enhanced through writings, mostly by missionaries, about Acholi language, history, customs, folktales, and proverbs.[4]

The missionary presence in Acholi introduced another fundamental change to the society: religious conversion. Religious affiliation was a central aspect of Ugandan colonial and decolonization politics, and the two major forces contesting power at the time of the nation's independence were divided along ethnic as well as religious lines: the largely Protestant south and the Catholic north. Religious affiliation also played an important role within internal Acholi politics, with eastern and western Acholi generally divided along the lines of the predominantly Protestant Uganda National Congress (UNC, later renamed Uganda Peoples' Congress [UPC]) and the Catholic Democratic Party (DP) (Paine 2014).

In Uganda, the British had fostered a bureaucratic elite from the south (especially from the kingdom of Buganda) while maintaining the inhabitants of the north as "a reservoir of labour" (Behrend 1999, 19). The postcolonial attempt at leveling this inequality through national unity was definitively abandoned in 1966, when Obote ordered an attack on the kabaka's palace and issued a new constitution that removed the kabaka as president, placed Obote as executive president, and banished monarchy federalism and all traditional political institutions from the country, forcing the kabaka into exile.

In 1971, Obote was overthrown in a military coup led by his commander in chief, Idi Amin, who was in turn overthrown in 1979 by a joint military offensive of the Tanzanian army and Ugandan exile groups living in Tanzania who had formed the Ugandan National Liberation Movement (UNLM) and Ugandan National Liberation Army (UNLA). Obote's controversial reinstatement to office in 1980—through what was alleged to be overt election fraud—caused a faction of the UNLA to break away and form the National Resistance Movement/Army (NRM/NRA) under the leadership of Yoweri Kaguta Museveni. This sparked the beginning of the bush war between the Ugandan UNLM/UNLA and Museveni's NRM and NRA (Allen 2010).

Among the many collective traumas caused by the bush war, one episode that stands out is the mass slaughter of thirty thousand civilians by UNLA soldiers in the central province of Luwero, as retribution for collaborating with the NRA. The fact that the UNLA was made up mainly of Nilotic-speaking soldiers, mostly from the Lango and Acholi regions of northern Uganda, while the NRA was made up mainly of Bantu-speaking Baganda and Banyankole fighters from southern Uganda and Banyarwanda further served to entrench the north–south divide that had already characterized Uganda's colonial politics.

In 1985, a group of Acholi officers from the UNLA overthrew President Milton Obote, and their leader, Tito Okello Lutwa, assumed the presidency of the country for six months (Allen 2010). A peace agreement was signed in Nairobi in 1985, which Museveni's NRA dismissed, resulting in the NRM's military takeover of the country in 1986. The new government began asserting its influence over Acholi, often through violent persecution of civilians, in what was repeatedly voiced as retaliation against the UNLA for the atrocities committed in Luwero (Allen 2006, 2010; Atkinson 2010a). Adam Branch perfectly summarizes the political crisis that engulfed Acholi society at that point in its history, and that led to the creation of various resistance groups in the region, the last of which was the Lord's Resistance Army (LRA): "After the NRA takeover in 1986, Acholi society was rent by two simultaneous, and related, political crises: an *internal* crisis stemming from the breakdown of authority within Acholi society . . . and a *national* crisis brought about by the destruction of the political links that had tied the Acholi in the district to the national state" (Branch 2010, 84).

Initially, the most important group resisting the NRA in Acholi was the Uganda People's Democratic Army (UPDA), made up largely of former UNLA soldiers. Another powerful resistance movement, formed in Kitgum, was the Holy Spirit Mobile Forces (HSMF) led by Alice Auma, who later took on the name Alice Lakwena after the spirit that had possessed her and endowed her with supernatural powers. Her ten thousand soldiers came from the UNLA and UPDA ranks and engaged the NRA in battle as far south as Iganga, where they were eventually defeated in October 1987 (Allen 2006). While many of the UNLA and UPDA fighters surrendered to the NRM in 1988, others refused the terms offered and regrouped under Joseph Kony, an emerging leader from Gulu rumored to be related to Alice Lakwena. After he was joined by Odong Latek, one of the most important ex-UPDA commanders who had refused to negotiate with the government, Kony's group became militarily organized as the Uganda People's Democratic Liberation Army (UPDLA). When Latek was killed in battle in 1990, Kony renamed his movement the Lord's Resistance Army (Ibid.). The emergence of these Acholi groups further contributed to isolating the region's inhabitants, with the majority of the Acholi population doubly alienated, both from the rebels, whom the majority of the population did not want to join, and from the central state that offered them neither protection nor a new political identity as citizens of the Ugandan nation (Branch 2010).

The political crises experienced in Acholiland were also sociocultural and religious in nature, as clearly illustrated in the important spiritual-religious dimension of both the HSMF and the LRA. Purification, cleansing, and spiritual redemption had been prerogatives of both Lakwena and Kony in their attempts to establish a support base across Acholi society, which was torn between the traditional authority of the elders and the small gains of a petty bourgeoise that had risen at the eve of independence but had been quickly crushed (Branch 2010). The Acholi thus found themselves caught between their ethnic and national identity, the latter never having had the time to fully develop, and the former constantly thrown back at them—from all parties to the conflict—as the only available identity. Amid these tense polarizations of social and political identities, the violence and frustration turned inward, as explained by Branch (2010, 128–29): "To this end, Kony invoked a language of Acholi identity as a way of asserting authority over a new potential constituency by framing the division between NRA collaborators and LRA supporters as a difference between false and genuine Acholi. . . . Part of Acholi would have to be fought as well, and so anti-civilian violence would be the privileged tool for carrying out this political programme. . . . The spiritual discourse of cleansing became one of violently expurgating the internal enemy from Acholi society." The spiritual discourse was strengthened by the fact that Kony said he was possessed by at least fourteen spirits, making him "nothing but the messenger ('laor'), who has no choice but to obey the spirits" (Titeca 2010, 187).

After a series of major atrocities committed by the LRA in the mid-1990s, such as the May 1995 Atiak massacre of three hundred people and the October 1996 Aboke girls' abduction from Lira, the government initiated a forced encampment policy such that by 2002 approximately 522,000 Acholis were living in IDP camps (Dolan 2009).

The government referred the case of northern Uganda to the International Criminal Court in December 2003, becoming the ICC's first case. By then, the number of Acholi who had been forced to move to

IDP camps had reached one and a half million people—over 90 percent of the Acholi population (Allen 2010; Atkinson 2010a). The plight of the Acholi had also started to reach international audiences after UN chief humanitarian officer Jan Egeland's visit to the region in 2005, when he described the situation in northern Uganda as "a human tragedy," "a moral outrage," and "the biggest neglected humanitarian emergency in the world" (quoted in Atkinson 2010a, 283).

Uganda's Judiciary

On July 14, 2006, just one year and a half after the ICC had issued arrest warrants, the Juba peace talks between the government and the LRA commenced, producing a first agenda item: a Cessation of Hostilities (CoH) Agreement that was signed on August 26 (Atkinson 2010b).

The peace talks were brokered by the newly autonomous South Sudan, which had an interest in pushing the LRA outside of its territory since the LRA had been receiving monetary and military support from the Sudanese government of Omar El Bashir. To gain US support, the Museveni government had emphasized Sudan's support of the LRA and presented the LRA as a terrorist organization backed by extremist Islamic supporters in Khartoum (Mwenda 2010). The creation of an autonomous South Sudan following the 2005 Comprehensive Peace Agreement (CPA) signed in Nairobi introduced a new element in the region's geopolitics, with the new South Sudanese vice president Riek Machar deeply involved in the negotiation talks and brokering peace between the LRA and Museveni.

The talks were suspended at the end of 2006 until May 2007, when Agenda Item Two, on comprehensive solutions to end the war and promote recovery and reconstruction, was signed (Atkinson 2010a). Agenda Item Three, on Accountability and Reconciliation (AAR), was signed on June 29, 2007. Following another six-month hiatus, the talks resumed in January 2008. Addenda to the major Agenda Items Two and Three were negotiated together with a final agenda item on Disarmament, Demobilization, and Reintegration (DDR), making the signing of a final peace deal seem imminent. However, Joseph Kony's failure to append his signature to the Final Peace Agreement (FPA, scheduled for November 29–30, 2008) brought the Juba peace process to an unresolved close (Ibid.). While the LRA boycotted the signing of the FPA, the government of Uganda on several occasions reaffirmed its commitment to implementing all other agreed-on agenda items. The AAR's implementation annex was signed in February 2008, providing the legal framework for the development of both a national transitional justice policy and a domestic war crimes division of the Ugandan High Court (Macdonald 2019).

In 2006, the Justice Law and Order Sector (JLOS) was created as a sector-wide approach to bring together institutions with closely linked mandates of administering justice and maintaining law and order and human rights. In 2008, JLOS established the Transitional Justice Working Group, a special policymaking entity tasked with developing a national policy and law on transitional justice for Uganda.[5] The Agreement on Accountability and Reconciliation and its annexure provide the legal framework for the drafting of the National Transitional Justice Policy (NTJP) by JLOS.[6]

Uganda operates under a common-law justice system wherein the courts of record are the Supreme Court, the Court of Appeal (which also doubles as the Constitutional Court), and the High Court. The subordinate courts include the Magistrates Court, Local Council Courts, and Qadi Courts (Callaghan 2009). The Judicature Act of 1996 constitutes the source of law—including statutory and case law, common law, doctrines of equity and customary law, and the constitution of 1995 (the third since independence)—as the supreme law of the country. The Local Council (LC) courts, originally called Resistance Councils (RCs), were established by the NRM in an effort to consolidate its power across the country by placing its representatives at the grassroots level to administer justice in the place of customary chiefs. The LC courts currently constitute the lowest level of the criminal justice system, with judicial powers at three levels: village (LCI), parish (LCII), and subcounty (LCIII). They can operate according to indigenous norms and customs (Robins 2009).

Robins (2009, 59) notes that the Ugandan justice system retains "an almost entirely retributive philosophy, consistent with its roots in English law," as demonstrated in the Judicature Act's limitation of customary law "in a language almost identical to that of the colonial penal code" (60): "Nothing in this Act shall deprive the High Court of the right to observe or enforce the observance of, or shall deprive any person of the benefit of, any existing custom, which is not repugnant to natural justice, equity and good conscience and not incompatible either directly or by necessary implication with any written law" (Republic of Uganda 1967).

According to Callaghan, the agreements that came out of Juba represented the most tangible experiment of legal pluralism in Uganda through their provision for the adoption of a range of justice mechanisms, including traditional justice (Callaghan 2009). In parallel to developing traditional and transitional justice, mainly through the work of the JLOS TJ working group, Uganda also domesticated the Rome Statute in 2010 and set up the International Crimes Division (ICD) in 2011, with a mandate to try cases of genocide, crimes against humanity, and war crimes. Suddenly, a legal inconsistency emerged between the Amnesty Act of 2000 and the ICC Act of 2010 in terms of who could or could not apply for amnesty. The most evident expression of this jurisprudential clash was the Thomas Kwoyelo trial, the first ever domestic trial for crimes against humanity conducted by the ICD of the Ugandan High Court.

The Amnesty Act of 2000 offered immunity to any Ugandan combatant who renounced involvement in war. Acholi religious and community leaders assiduously pursued amnesty, especially under the leadership of the Acholi Religious Leaders Peace Initiative (ARLPI) and the Acholi Parliamentary Group (Bradfield 2017). The Ugandan amnesty ended up being one of the largest applications of modern amnesty in Africa, with twenty-seven thousand ex-combatants benefiting from the process, seven thousand of who were reintegrated into their communities (Republic of Uganda, National Transitional Justice Policy 2019, 3).

There was no specific exemption for the LRA leadership in Uganda's original amnesty law, but the year after the ICC indictments, the law was amended to allow the interior minister to seek parliamentary approval to exclude certain individuals from receiving amnesty. In 2010, the minister asked parliament to exclude four LRA fighters: Joseph Kony, Dominic Ongwen, Okoto Odhiambo, and Thomas Kwoyelo. The motion did not pass, and a blanket amnesty remained in place for all acts and all actors "engaged in war or armed rebellion against the Government of the Republic of Uganda" (Republic of Uganda, Amnesty Act 2000).

However, in 2009 LRA combatant Thomas Kwoyelo—who had been abducted from school by the LRA when he was thirteen years old—was charged by the DPP with twelve counts of violations of the Geneva convention and committed to the ICD to await trial. Soon after

Kwoyelo's trial commenced on July 11, 2011, the Constitutional Court of Uganda issued a ruling that the trial should stop as the court found no reasonable grounds for the DPP and the Amnesty Commission's failure to act on Kwoyelo's application. On November 23, 2011, Kwoyelo filed a complaint with the Ugandan High Court in Kampala, requesting to be amnestied. The DPP denied his request in February 2012 and appealed to the Supreme Court (Porter and Macdonald, 2016).

On April 8, 2015, the Supreme Court denied Kwoyelo's amnesty application and allowed his trial to resume (Bradfield 2017). The trial is now in the defense stage; Thomas Kwoyelo faces more than seventy charges including murder, rape, and the recruitment of child soldiers (Booty and Ibrahim, 2024).

In May 2012, while Kwoyelo's application for amnesty was proceeding, the government let Part II of the Amnesty Act lapse; this was controversial and raised strong reactions from Ugandan civil society organizations. Under the pressure of a sustained and cohesive lobbying action by many Ugandan NGOs, CSOs, and CBOs, the government agreed to reinstate Part II of the Amnesty Act. While strongly advocating for the reinstatement, Ugandan civil society organizations were also advocating for the development of a comprehensive transitional justice policy that would harmonize the scattered judicial landscape of the country and ensure justice for victims. The policy was finalized in 2019, but it is yet to translate into concrete action as a transitional justice bill is still being developed.

So far, the finalization of the NTJP has not led to a large-scale application of traditional justice processes, and the use of ATJMs has remained more or less circumscribed to small-scale independent community initiatives without much government involvement. At the time of my research, for example, in the absence of clear legislation regulating their use, traditional justice approaches in response to the conflict in Acholi were undertaken mainly either as independent initiatives by certain communities or by NGOs, often in partnership with the cultural institution Ker Kwaro Acholi (KKA). Ker Kwaro Acholi was set up in 2000 under the terms of Article 246 of the 1995 Ugandan constitution, which allows for the institution of traditional or cultural leaders (Allen 2010). In 2004, Kenneth Oketta was appointed prime minister of KKA, and in 2005 a public coronation ceremony of rwot Acana was conducted, attended by President Museveni. At the time of its creation, KKA was made up of rwodi from the fifty-two officially recognized chiefdoms under the overall authority of the paramount chief, an executive council comprising nineteen chiefs and elders, a youth representative, and two female representatives (Baines 2005).

Allen reports that by mid-2005, "dozens of *mato oput* ceremonies were being performed, with Acholi paramount chief also performing larger-scale public rituals" (Allen 2010, 687). According to Latigo, the United States Aid for International Development (USAID)–funded Northern Uganda Peace Initiative Programme (NUPI) supported KKA in the performance of fifty-four mato oput ceremonies between 2004 and 2006 (Latigo 2008).

In order to to assess the social impact of these ceremonies, in 2005 Tim Allen's research team created a sample of formerly abducted people who had returned from the LRA ranks and located 238 of them. The team gathered that all of them were living in displacement camps or in the main towns in the war zone, that none of them had performed mato oput, and that only sixty-nine had been involved in any kind of reconciliation ceremony (Allen 2010, 693). The team's findings thus suggest that traditional justice practices were not having a major impact on the reintegration of LRA returnees.

While I did not conduct any quantitative surveys to investigate the impact of the use of Acholi traditional justice mechanisms in the postwar context, the many in-depth dialogues I conducted across Acholiland on the significance of Acholi justice mechanisms, as well as the many civil society engagements I participated in as an intern for the Refugee Law Project and the ICC Review Conference I participated in as a member of the Italian delegation to the ICC, constantly brought me face to face with the cause of the Acholi quest for justice in their own traditional terms as a powerful cause that was made to resonate nationally and internationally.

Acholi Traditional Justice Mechanisms

One of the most thorough categorizations and descriptions of Acholi justice practices is that by Harlacher et al. (2006), though the authors do not refer to them as justice mechanisms but rather as healing ceremonies, which they divide into two categories: "rituals related to the receiving of returnees back home" (65) and "rituals with a focus on conflict resolution" (74).

Under the first category, they place *nyono tonggweno* (stepping on the egg) and *lwoko pik wang* (washing away the tears), which are conducted for the welcoming and initial cleansing of returnees who have been away from the community for a long time. Other returnee-welcoming ceremonies gathered in this study include *moyo tipu* (cleansing the spirit)—the last funeral rites for people who have died in the wilderness—and *moyo piny*, which is a general cleansing ritual for specific areas, similar to another ceremony called *moyo kom*. *Kwero merok* is the cleansing of someone who has killed in war, which traditionally was not applied to someone who killed members of the family or clan, while *ryemo jok* is the chasing away of a free *jok*, or spirit that has possessed someone.[7]

Under conflict resolution rituals, Harlacher et al. (2006) include *tumu kir* (cleansing for a taboo committed), *mato oput* (drinking oput), and *gomo tong* (bending of spears).[8] *Tumu kir* is employed to cleanse in the face of events that are considered *kir* (taboo), that displease or insult ancestors and chiefdom *joggi*, and that may result in the occurrence of misfortunes. Gomo tong was traditionally performed to mark the end of a war between different Acholi clans or chiefdoms or between Acholi and foreign communities (Harlacher et al. 2006).

The Acholi justice practice that has most come to embody and represent Acholi traditional justice as a whole is mato oput, due to its inclusion in the Agreement on Accountability and Reconciliation, which has put it at the center of the justice debate, as well as its documentation by international NGOs, academics, and media.[9] The literal translation of *mato oput* is "drinking the bitter root"; it is a ritual marking the peak of a conflict resolution process following a killing that has occurred in the community. It was traditionally not applied to killings in war but to both premeditated and accidental killings between friendly clans in times of peace to reestablish relationships between the clans that had been suspended (Harlacher et al. 2006).[10] It was usually carried out after a long process of mediation and was characterized by the willingness of the offender clan to assume responsibility for the act as well as their readiness and ability to pay compensation (*culo kwor*). According to Okumu, the first written account of these Acholi practices is Italian missionary Renato Boccassino's 1962 article for *Anthropos* bearing the derogatory title "The Blood Vengeance Practiced by the Acholi of Uganda: Rituals and War Cannibalism" (my translation), which mobilizes all the cultural and racial stereotypes of the time, referring to the African continent as a land of cannibalism and war.[11] It is not even clear what Bocassino means by cannibalism here, if it is blood vengeance or something else. The reason Okumu referred me to this article is because here Boccassino transcribes narrations by two Acholi elders in which reference is made to payment of compensation between two clans for an accidental killing during hunting. Boccassino calls the compensation *nyako kwor*, which was in the form of a girl (or two) from the offender clan to the offended clan so that she/they may marry and generate new life to replace the one that was taken (Boccassino 1962). This is what Ochieng refers to as the symbolism of "child salvation," embodied in the offering of a young girl to the bereaved community so that "her presence becomes a bridge between the two communities."[12]

This form of compensation is no longer in use and was apparently stopped under British colonialism, so *culo kwor* is now only in the form of animals, money, or symbolic compensation during times of economic hardship. The literal meaning of *culo kwor*, "to pay life," is maintained in the sense that the money or animals paid to the offended party are used to seal the dowry payment of one of its clan members so he may marry and, with his wife, generate a new life to replace the one that was lost because of the conflict.[13] Boccassino never explicitly refers a ceremony called *mato oput* in his article, and neither does Girling, who describes it as "the reconciliation ceremony after killing" (Girling 1960, 67).

Relating the different ceremonies to Acholi social and political structures, Father Joseph Okumu explains how the different levels of Acholi social stratification—classified by Girling as the household, hamlet, village, and domain—inform specific ritual ceremonies of reconciliation so that cleansing rituals such as *tumu kir* are used at the household and hamlet levels while at the other three levels the rites of *mato oput* or *gomo tong* are applied (Okumu 2009). It is clear, then, that traditionally, levels of responsibility and the associated accountability measures were significantly related both to the type of social relation between the offender and the offended party and to the status of property. Since livestock formed part of the common wealth of the village, the demand of compensation that was required for mato oput would have amounted to "merely taking something out of the right hand and putting it into the left" (Girling 1960, 67) among members of the same village, which is why the ritual was mostly performed between members from different villages.

Furthermore, for the killing of an agnate, the performance of the ceremony known as *tum* (cleansing) was essential because the killing was considered an offense against the ancestors (Girling 1960). This type of wrongdoing is generally referred to as *kir*, which is most often translated as "taboo," though p'Bitek (1971) also translates it as "curse." The commission of kir is not only the violation of a social rule but also an offense to the ancestors who safeguard the rules of society and who could bestow misfortune and illness on the living if these were violated (Harlacher at al. 2006).

Lajul explains that traditionally these different levels of accountability related to diverse attributions of responsibility: tumu kir was the personal reparation for wrongdoing committed by an individual standing in representation of himself/herself while during mato oput the whole clan stood in representation of the wrongdoer and assumed responsibility for his/her/their actions.[14] What is key to understanding these different layers of responsibility is that the community-based collective responsibility entailed in mato oput can be taken on only *after* the offender's recounting of the events that led to a killing and following his/her/their *personal* ownership of the wrong. This was expressed by two elders: "Somebody must own the crime. Somebody must confess to the crime. The offender must accept the crime was committed. Then the mediators bring them together."[15] After this initial individual confession, the community of the perpetrator begins referring to his/her/their wrong as "ours," as explained by Oola:

> So what happens is that I confess. I come to my immediate family, maybe to my father, and I say, "daddy I have done this. I have mistakenly or otherwise killed somebody." And the father will say, "no! That is bad!" He then goes to the clan, to his immediate clan members, and says: "our son has done a grave thing: he has killed somebody." The clan now takes it over. They are not going to say: "Oola has killed somebody." I am now not only my father's son. They will say, "our son has killed." They begin to own up to it. As a clan they sit down and say: "We have done this bad thing. How do we correct it?" Because it will have strained relationships between the offender and the bereaved clan, the offenders will send an emissary to say: "We

want to confess, our son has done this to you. What do we do?" And then they begin to negotiate.[16]

Rt. Rev. MacBaker Ochola identifies the main ingredients of mato oput: personal testimony at the gate; *nyono-tonggweno* (stepping on the egg); the offender being kept in confinement or isolation; community-based collective responsibility; and finally the actual ceremony of drinking the oput. According to the first "ingredient" of mato oput:

> The offender is not allowed to enter into the village with the blood of his or her crime in his/her hands. He/she was expected to stand outside the gate, testify against himself or herself to the people or the community in the village. He/she first must tell his or her own name, his/her mother's, father's and uncle's name. This means his or her identity must be given unambiguously to all in the village. . . . The personal testimony also includes confession of motive for the homicide committed. The offender must also give the name, gender, and clan of the person killed and why he/she was killed. (Ochola 2014, 16–17)

Following the personal testimony, if the offender's community members are convinced of his/her/their account, the elders of the village assume full collective responsibility on behalf of the offender by performing the ritual of nyono-tonggweno, which is also carried out at the gate of the village as soon as the personal testimony is given by the offender. This ritual is rich in its symbolic references to "acceptance of the offender as still a member of the community in spite of the serious crimes committed, and the shame and disgrace brought upon the entire community of the clan; purity and sanctity of human life which has been destroyed by the Offender; and destruction of human life which the community accepts as an act of murder, a violation of the sanctity of human life and an abomination" (Ochola 2014, 18).

At first the offender is not allowed to return to his/her/their family but is kept in confinement and isolation within the fence of the village for a specific period in order to "show the seriousness of the violation and desecration of the sanctity of human life. It is a time of reflection and re-examination for the Offender" (Ochola 2014, 18). The offender community is at this point under obligation and responsibility to urgently inform the offended community about the murder of one of its dear members. They do this through a third-party community, to which a formal request is made to play the role of arbitrator between the offender and the offended communities. Ochola identifies the main elements of the actual mato oput procedure that follow these first ingredients: truth telling, payment of compensation, the ritual of sharing food between the offender and offended communities, and finally the ritual of drinking bitter herbs.

James Ojera Latigo similarly describes the process leading up to mato oput as well as the ceremony itself, with the interesting and quite unique inclusion of the invocations uttered throughout the process, which prove highly interesting for philosophical analysis. Latigo (2008, 103) describes the suspension of all relations between members of the two clans once the killing has happened in terms of a "supernatural barrier [that] remains in force until the killing is atoned for and a religious rite of reconciliation has been performed, to cleanse the taint." He also stresses the initial ostracizing of the killer on behalf of his or her own community due to "fear that he is a companion of the evil spirits which constituted the *ujabu* and will pollute the soil of the homestead with the evil spirits."[17] He then goes on to provide a detailed description of the actual mato oput ceremony:

> After the payment of the money (reparation), the elders arrange for the customary rite of reconciliation to take place in order to bring the estranged clans together to resume a normal working relationship. The reconciliation ceremony always takes place in an uncultivated field which is usually somewhere between the villages or communal settlements of the two clans, away from any footpath or any place commonly frequented by women and children.
>
> To perform the reconciliation ceremony, the killer provides a ram and a bull (*dyang me dog bur*), while the next of kin of the person killed provides a goat. Unused new vessels are required and a large quantity of beer is brewed for the occasion. On the appointed day, the traditional masters of ceremony, conciliators and elders from both clans, assemble at the chosen site and stand facing westwards in solemn silence. An invocation is then performed which sums up the entire spirit and intent of reconciliation.

The master of ceremonies' invocation:

You our ancestors and the children of the Supreme Deity! I now plead with you and ask you to realize that sin is part of man's life. It was started by those who ever lived before us. This man whose fault brought us here today has merely repeated the perennial SIN which man has hitherto failed to discard since time immemorial. He killed his own brother. But since then he has repented of his evil deed. He has paid blood money which may be used to marry a woman who will produce children who, in turn, will keep the name of his killed brother for our posterity. We now beseech you our ancestors to let the two families resume a brotherly relationship.

All the assembled elders join in and chant together: "Let a man who will be given the blood money to marry a wife be sharp and pick on a vivacious woman . . . a virgin woman who will produce many and healthy children to grow up well and take over the empty home."

Another master of ceremonies from the clan of the killed person responds to the solemn invocation in the following terms: "We are not the first clan to suffer premature death of this kind. The killer has repented his misdeed. He has paid for it. We now supplicate you our ancestors to bless the blood money given to the family to marry a wife to produce a replacement for our killed brother."

All the assembled elders join the invocation and chant together: "Let us accept the blood money and wash our hearts clean, and begin to live and work together as we have been doing in the past. . . . Our enemies who have heard of this reconciliation and are not happy that it will now bring peace and prosperity to our two clans. . . . Let their ill will be carried away by the sun to the west, and sink with it down, deep and deep down" (Latigo 2008, 104).

Although traditionally the communal participation in culo kwor was one of the central aspects of the community-based collective responsibility principle underlying the entire mato oput process, according to Okello, it is now falling out of use because of "individualism, privatization, and property ownership."[18] Furthermore, the possibility of neatly framing a community member's wrongful action as "inside" or "outside" a particular village is currently defied by the changed sociopolitical and geographical circumstances, with almost 90 to 95 percent of the Acholi population living in IDP camps at the height of the conflict, the widespread degree of participation in LRA crimes across Acholiland—whether voluntary or forced—and intensive urbanization and migration processes in the region. These population movements have undoubtedly challenged the traditional village demarcations and thus also pose new challenges to the way different levels of responsibility for different types of wrongs are conceptualized.

Another important factor that has posed a great challenge to the applicability of traditional notions of responsibility to the postwar context is the type of wrongs that were committed during the conflict, which are very commonly referred to as *new crimes* characterized by a level, nature, and scale of atrocity that defy historical memory, together with the novel circumstance presented by the high degree of civilian involvement in the commission of such crimes, whether voluntary or forced. While there is a widespread sense that the types of wrongs committed in the war present an aspect of novelty for which there is no precedent in Acholi, most of the interlocutors of this book easily related them to the Acholi moral vocabulary of *ujebu*, indicating "something that is morally dirty and unbecoming," and *bal*, indicating "sin," or *bal ujebu*, "contagious sin."[19] One historian indicates the meaning of *bal* to be "abomination" and renders both *labal* and *lajok* as "the one who commits immoral behavior," the latter of which is also used by p'Bitek (1971) to denote witches.[20] Porter explains the etymological root of *bal* as "breaking," whereas labal is the one who breaks social harmony.[21] Also important is the notion of kir (curse or curse casting) as the result of wrongdoing by community members.

Still, the presence of these new crimes creates a divergence of opinions regarding the desirability and possibility of applying traditional justice mechanisms today. Many have posed the question of responsibility for mass crimes as a new phenomenon that lacks a historical accountability mechanism to refer to in the traditional justice framework (Baines 2007). Baines (2007, 105) has highlighted how the numerous elders she interviewed across Acholiland almost universally expressed the opinion that there was "little sense in pursuing *mato oput* on a case-by-case basis, as too many people had been killed and it was therefore difficult to trace who had killed whom and which clans to engage." For others, applying ATJMs to the post–northern Ugandan war context does present challenges, but they are challenges that can be overcome. In this overcoming, the tradition must be adapted to meet the demands of current situations. Harlacher et al. (2006, 80), for example, maintain that "given the current sense of a common Acholi identity extending across all of Acholiland, the procedure is most likely applicable between any of the Acholi clans."

The ARLPI, an interfaith peace-building and conflict-transformation organization, has been one of the most proactive groups in the north in advocating for the Amnesty Act 2000, consulting for the Juba peace talks, and generally striving toward nonviolent solutions to end the war and to foster peace among affected communities. ARLPI has also been at the forefront of articulating the use of traditional justice in Acholi. According to Ocen (2015, 6), "The ARLPI never advocated for retributive justice because of the mixed-up composition of former combatants that included formerly abducted children, mothers, abducted NGO workers, and women." Attempts to adapt the tradition to this new context have been carried out mainly by KKA in what have been commonly referred to as communal or collective cleansing ceremonies.

While criticisms to adaptations of Acholi traditional restorative rituals to deal with crimes against humanity come from all corners of the intellectual debate, ranging from Western academics to Acholi advocates of TJMs, the camp tends to be divided between those refuting altogether the desirability and/or applicability of such mechanisms and those tending to be more conciliatory in their concession that tradition *can* be adapted to new instances of criminality—such as those entailed in the perpetration of mass atrocities and crimes against humanity—as long as the aspects that are considered *essential* to Acholi justice are not compromised, such as the acceptance of communally based collective responsibility, the full disclosure of the truth, and the undergoing of the actual ritual process. Virtually all interlocutors of this book described a concept constituting the Acholi justice paradigm par excellence—what Ochola (2014, 17) calls "community-based collective responsibility"—which is the sharing of responsibility for a community member's wrongdoing by other members of his/her/their community. This relates both to the understanding of the deep issues that caused conflict as well as to the appropriate redress mechanisms that need to be mobilized in order to right the wrongs committed, which in the context of the northern war have been categorized as crimes against humanity by both the ICC and the Juba peace talks.

3 Community-Based Collective Responsibility

In the aftermath of the war, a context that was described as one where "virtually no one remains untouched by the violence" (Atkinson 2010a, 283), many spoke of the deep causes of the mass violence in Acholiland as concerning the entire Acholi community and surroundings (*piny*), which included nonliving and nonhuman members such as kwari (who inhabit abila), *joggi*, tipu, and cen. This is what Ochola (2014) defines as community-based collective responsibility, which is the sharing of responsibility for a community member's wrongdoing by other members of his/her/their community. This concept was described by virtually all of the interlocutors of this book as constituting the traditional paradigm par excellence that renders Acholi approaches to justice inherently different from Western approaches centered on notions of individual liability.

The ethical foundation of community-based collective responsibility is identified by Joyce with "the African norm of humanity, of togetherness" that is reflected in the communal ownership over wrongdoing because "we are one and if someone commits a crime or if one of us is at fault all of us have to support them," a principle that she believes "clearly comes out in the South African norm of *ubuntu*."[1] The ontological foundation of community-based collective responsibility is explained by Okumu as the conception of being in relational terms:

> That is why I think that at the ontological level—the level of being— then you ask: "Who is the individual?" If you don't understand it in relational terms you will never understand it. Ontologically it is like the individual disappears into the communal and then the communal also mutually disappears into the individual. Hence the saying: "I am because we are and we are because I am." So one is causing the other: the individual is causing the community and the community is causing the individual. It's such a strong concept of interrelation.

I don't know even whether sometimes it's close to . . . I am thinking of the ideas of Heraclitus: the idea of change and of flux; everything in a state of flux. *But* at the same time there is a permanence with the people.[2]

Okumu's ontological foundation of the ethical norm of togetherness as underlying the concept of community-based collective responsibility in a justice process is emphasized also by Daniel Komakech (2012, 134), who applies Placide Tempels's philosophical framework to that of the Acholi: "In Acholi, ontology is not conceived in the transcendental aspect by separating being from its attribute, 'force.' Force, as rightly observed by Tempels, is a necessary element in being, and the concept of 'force' is inseparable from the definition of being. Second, beings are bound together and preserve a bond with one another, an intimate ontological relationship. Thus, the Western concept of a being as 'being as such,' namely being entirely independent of one another, is foreign to Acholi thought."

In this binding together of beings, suffering too is shared across the community, with jok, abila, and cen as expressions of that. What I found in the course of my research was that both the causes and the effects of the war and violence were discussed in terms of *responsibility*. The ascertainment of the scale of suffering that enveloped Acholi collectivity was accompanied by a sense of collective responsibility.

Many interlocutors spoke of the Acholi people as a whole being morally responsible for creating an environment in which atrocities among Acholis took place or for having turned their backs on their abila in favor of foreign religions, thus stirring the wrath of the ancestors that made themselves manifest through Joseph Kony's spirit possession and his infliction of devastation among the Acholi. They also spoke of the legacy of mass crimes indiscriminately afflicting community members regardless of whether they participated directly in the commission of those crimes.

Sharing the blame across the Acholi people as a whole for Kony's acts was voiced in many of the dialogues I had, in which my interlocutors referred to him as "our child" and expressed a sense of answerability for his deeds as members of his same community who should have ensured his development into an "upright person," especially since the notion of *child* in Acholi culture applies to all members of the community irrespective of their age.[3] Some also referred to the initial blessing that Kony received from the elders when he began his resistance against the government as implicating them as well.[4] "When he [Joseph Kony] was growing up in his village there was I, the uncle; I, the aunt; I, the nephew; I, the mother; I, the father; I, the brother—we were all there so why did we not do our best to help him grow up well? In some way we all contributed to the formation of his personality, which then ended up causing so much damage."[5]

When responsibility is framed in terms of jok, abila and cen, a holistic notion of responsibility is produced where the focus is not strictly on individual agency and action but on the wider environment within which the individual wrongdoer is operating and the circumstantial conditions that affect him/her/them.

This holistic notion of responsibility is profoundly connected to the Acholi justice process, which Onyango Odongo described as a process that should not "bring suffering on top of suffering" (*cian kom wadei*), as this would never benefit society.[6] Cian kom wadei is the opposite of ngol matir or ngol ma opore, for it does not look for a way forward by creating a win-win situation where all parties are content and where balance is restored. This does not mean that the individual wrongdoer is not liable for his/her/their actions but that those actions and the reparations they entail have to be understood as a more complex whole for justice to be achieved.

Jok

Jok is often described as the direct cause of wrongful acts. Though jok possesses individual persons, the emergence and possession of jok is often the result of the person's wider environment.

In the context of the northern Uganda war, it is important to remember that both leaders of the Acholi Holy Spirit Mobile Forces (HSMF) and LRA militia groups—Alice Lakwena and Joseph Kony, respectively—were spirit mediums (*ajwaki*), though Lakwena differentiated herself from the traditional Acholi ajwaki by self-identifying instead as *nebi*, which has been interpreted by some as an expression of her Catholic faith *against* traditional Acholi spiritual beliefs (Allen 1991).[7] Joseph Kony also claimed to be possessed by foreign joggi and linked himself even more explicitly with Christianity, regarding himself as a prophet of the Holy Spirit, though he also drew inspiration from Islam (Allen 2006). Kony rejected Acholi "paganism" and, as part of his manifesto, envisioned the coming into being of a new Acholi people who would distance themselves from the old "impure" Acholi ways (Baines 2010).

The relevance of the religious/spiritual transformations that had been taking shape in Acholi culture since the arrival of the first missionaries can be clearly observed in the founding principles of these militia leaders, who, as Allen (1991, 370) points out, "have been possessed not by ancestral ghosts but by strangers." The phenomenon of possession by free joggi—that is, not ancestral lineage joggi—was being highlighted by p'Bitek (1970, 112) already in the 1970s as a significant phenomenon in Acholi: "In northern Uganda the chiefdom deities perished during the first few years of colonial rule. Today there are many young men and women who know nothing about them. The cult of the ancestors is still strong, and this reflects the continuing bond of relationship between members of a clan. The numerous *jogi*, spirits, which are believed to be the cause of diseases and other misfortunes, appear to be on the increase."[8]

This observation has been corroborated by other researchers such as Behrend (1999, 107), who notes an increasing tendency since the colonial period of chiefdom and clan joggi to generally fade into the background while "the free *joggi* and the witches gained even more power." Harlacher et al. (2006, 48) also note that with the spread of Christianity in the region, "the reverence towards clan and chiefdom *joggi* seems to have almost died out" while the free joggi "increased strongly in number and influence during and after the colonial era."

Explanations for the causes of jok possession vary, from being very tangible and traceable to being completely random and unexplainable. In *Religion of the Central Luo* (1971), p'Bitek often discusses the phenomenon and gives multiple examples of different types of jok possession. There is a particularly evocative passage in which p'Bitek describes jok possession as something that can happen to anyone for unknown reasons:

> The *la-jok* [witch] was irresistibly forced by the witchcraft in him to do evil things. He did not bewitch a person for any particular reason, but acted blindly. He was not malicious, and the harmful activities

that he did were not of any benefit to himself or his family; indeed he often suffered the consequences. Witchcraft power was then regarded as something akin to extreme anger, overwhelming fear or lunacy which affected the normal behaviour of individuals. And the idea that the witch was a victim of an irresistible power which dazed his eyes and made him do certain acts which, when normal, he would not do, partly explains the mixed feelings of the Luo towards witches. He was both feared and pitied. . . . So in some cases he was tolerated in the same way that an insane person was tolerated. Hence the very mild punishments that were meted out. (p'Bitek 1971, 123)

Although here p'Bitek insists on the mild punishments that were meted out to witches, we find other passages of his work (quoted later in this chapter) where he describes brutal punishments inflicted on witches, thus testifying to two very different circumstantial reactions to what appears to be the same type of wrong.

p'Bitek describes jok as taking over an individual, causing him/her/them to perform certain acts, even to his/her/their own detriment. Traces of p'Bitek's explanation of jok or lajok as causes of wrongdoing can be found in the following excerpt from my dialogue with Okumu where he makes the same reference to spirit possession as the ultimate bearer of responsibility for what are classified as inhumane actions: "For example, looking at you and casting a spell in your eyes and making you blind. A *jok* inside me causes me to cast this spell and makes me cause evil to you. . . . Many times we think, when someone drinks and beats his wife so many times, what the people believe is that he has bad spirits in him that possessed him and make him beat the wife. When an act becomes so much repeated in the person it becomes projected as a spirit living."[9]

From these accounts, jok can appear to be the ultimate bearer of responsibility in a manner that removes any sense of individual accountability for acts committed. However, this would not be an accurate interpretation in my view, as removal of individual accountability would never be conducive to a successful justice process, where the rituals involving individual ownership of wrongful deeds are crucial. The point of talking about responsibility in terms of jok is to understand the wrongful actions committed by an individual as embedded in a wider environment that affects him/her/them. From Okumu's interpretation it is clear "you are still seen as responsible for the action." However, much attention is paid to the fact that "your actions" are committed in a wider environment that influences you "in a way you cannot exist without these spiritual things. Through your ancestors, through your great-great-grandfathers—remember this hierarchy of beings in Africa, even that Mbiti talks about. The beings, inanimate, animate and how they relate to humans, the trees and all, how they all interrelate to the human person in a very concrete way. And so they can really take possession of the human person. And it's so intense and so intrinsic that they can really cause the person to [act]."[10]

The different interpretations of jok in Acholi and Luo traditions give rise to completely different moral philosophies that carry very different notions of responsibility, which have a direct bearing on ideas and philosophies of justice. While in some interpretations of jok morality/immorality and criminal acts are described as mandated by a spiritual being over which the human agent has verry little power, there exists another philosophical interpretation of jok that casts the phenomenon as an almost metaphoric rendering of a profoundly human-centered experience where joggi feature as depictions of mental states or life occurrences. Situated in this second interpretative framework is, for example, Masolo's (2012, 185) reading of jok as "a moral concept that seeks to idealize social virtues":

> The various chiefdom *jok* name the various ancestors with whom members of some chiefly lineages identify. Their *jok* status is associated with mass deaths that were the result of war and other large-scale calamities, such as epidemics. To these one can add the *jok nam* (the *jok* of the river or lake), the *jok kulo* (the *jok* of the pond), the *jok thim* (the *jok* of the wilderness), and so on. These refer to the lingering identities of those who may have met their deaths in these places, some by accident, others as a result of war or suicide. Their bodies were not recovered for proper rituals and burial. The Luo believe that people who take their lives in anger or who die as victims of mistreatment by family "conceal" their remains from recovery but can be heard singing their lamentations when people visit or pass by the places where they died. They become *jok* (or *juogi*) of those locations. When they avenge their unfair deaths they become *chien* and torment the conscience of the culprits. In this sense, *jok* is a category of the mind—that is, it refers to mental content, a memory (as in historical knowledge) that people carry with them for generations and from which they infer a variety of moral and emotional awareness. (Masolo 2010, 193)

These divergent interpretations of jok have a central bearing on ideas of responsibility and justice because of the moral philosophies that unravel from them and will be analyzed in detail in the last section of this chapter on personhood.

Abila

Notions of responsibility change when attributed in terms of abila with respect to those attributed in terms of jok, entailing a higher degree of guilt. This is clearly explained by Harlacher et al. (2006, 114): "The striking difference between the diseases attributed to the free *jok*, and those caused by ancestral spirits is that with the latter, guilt was a dominant factor. The ancestors were angry because they had been neglected, because somebody among the living had not done his or her duty. With the free *jok*, on the other hand, there was no apparent cause for their attack."

Responsibility in terms of abila takes two main forms: neglect of ancestors by their living descendants, which causes the ancestors to retaliate; and repercussions on the living from their ancestors' wrongful actions, per the following account by Okumu:

> So that for example someone can die not because he has done anything, but because the ancestors committed something, and so the fathers become the cause of the death of the child. . . . The child remains innocent but the guilty one is the father or the mother or the uncle or the sister. And so he [the child] pays for that . . . because [we] belong to those ancestors, we are part of that ancestry—we are because of them; they caused us to be. So if you forget them, you stop them from being in the *now*—the *hic et nunc*.[11]

Another elder also referred to this phenomenon in similar terms:

> We have a belief that you cannot commit evil and nothing completely happens to you. If it is true that you have committed evil, sometimes you may not be there to see the results, but your sons and grandsons will pay for it. And right now, in Acholiland, I think people are paying for it. During the insurgency people committed evil. When we asked people who were returning: "Come and tell us any wrong thing that you could have done during the insurgency so we can see what we can do about it." Some people told us, some people kept quiet. You are now seeing very many people running mad in the town. They were not mad. Young people, good people,

you know they look innocent. So sometimes it doesn't play out exactly in that person. For example, somebody could have committed evil and he died. It will take some bit of time and the children will pay for it.[12]

Unlike jok, ancestral spirits are rarely described as the direct agents of wrong but rather as the incarnation of wrongs committed by humans that have not been accounted for. Persons who become "possessed" by the ancestral spirits are often described as *already* morally compromised, although that moral compromise is in turn described in terms of having something wrong with one's abila. This creates a kind of circle whereby the abila spirits possess you if you are behaving immorally, and yet you are behaving immorally because of your abila. This phenomenon is well described in the two following accounts, one from my own dialogues in the region and one taken from an interview that Tim Allen conducted with an *ajwaka,* presumably in the early 2000s. "If your *abila* is good and not tarnished by blood, your hand should not dig itself into somebody's blood. But if there is evil in your domestic community, the evil force will influence *you*. So that extra-ordinary force, that extra-evil force, which causes you to sin, uses your history, uses your geography, uses your environment, uses your own way of doing things."[13] "The spirits are influenced by the individual's own character. . . . Once a spirit comes over someone it only gives the person the power to do their heart's desires. Therefore, Kony had something wrong with his ancestral spirits and thus the spirits that came over him made him do the evil things" (quoted in Allen 2006, 159–60).

What is extremely important is that in both of these accounts, the individual is defined in terms of his/her/their ancestral spirits so that in fact there is no individual dimension of being that is separate from these other beings; the ancestors of the abila are not separate/external from the living community member but rather constitutive of that living community member's ontological and moral personhood.

Cen

Another key recurring being that features in elaborations of wrongdoing and community-based collective responsibility is cen. In the work of p'Bitek, cen is described as a vengeance ghost, usually belonging to someone whose murder has been unaccounted for. Harlacher et al. (2006, 60) specify that the haunting of cen is "not restricted only to people who have killed or have kinship relations to the killer" because "*cen* can also be contracted just by finding a person who has died a violent death or passing through an area where killings have taken place."

It is precisely the explanation of the haunting or possession of cen as *not* necessarily related to individual wrongdoing that informs my interpretation of the phenomenon as entailing a concept of responsibility that is the concrete manifestation of suffering, which inevitably comes to affect a community in which a wrong has been committed, regardless of who the perpetrator is. According to this notion of responsibility, the focus is not on the determination of guilt or innocence but on the community members' duty to repair the damage that has occurred, whether or not they were directly involved in committing it.

When the damage is so widespread and the suffering so pervasive, as in the Acholi postwar scenario, the utmost priority is to address the effects of wrongdoing that are indiscriminately affecting community members—regardless of their direct participation in the commission of wrongful acts—rather than the apportionment of individualized culpability. This is also because the participation in the crimes committed was so widespread and so complex, involving minors, abductees, and other subjects whose agency in committing the crimes was so hard to establish, as Porter explained well: "*Cen* is something that happens involuntarily and it can happen whether you are guilty or innocent. . . . It usually happens because *somebody* is guilty. Maybe you yourself are not guilty but it's because a spirit is angered and something happened to make that spirit angry. Some guilty act, some wrong."[14]

In the postwar scenario, cen inhabited the lands and the homes of the Acholi, to the point of making their return from the camps impossible without cleansing ceremonies by the *rwodi* and priests.[15] This clearly constitutes an extreme scenario where the cause and the culprits of the violence were so widespread and wide reaching that cen was all pervasive. Cen, however, also appears in quotidian Acholi life and in relation to specific actions by community members that are clearly identifiable. p'Bitek, for example, mentions "the fierce vengeance ghost" in connection to the phenomenon of curse casting (kir), which he describes as an extreme gesture committed by someone forced into an intolerable position by another member of the community, such as in the case of a wife who is mistreated by her husband:

> When a wife, because of extreme anger and frustration, deliberately took a pot or dish, with or without food in it, or scooped ash from the cooking stove (*keno*) and threw it out, this act was called *twacco kir*. And as she threw the pot, or dish, she said,
>
> > *Uyaa! An mono pe adano?*
> > Oh! Am I not a human being?
>
> . . . As soon as the *kir* was committed, the attitudes of the people towards the woman changed. While before they sympathised with her in her troubles, now they began to blame her, and she felt guilty and ashamed. But the blame was tempered by the thought that she was forced to do the act, and also by the consideration that she might have committed suicide as an alternative, and this would have been an even worse step, as she would become a fierce vengeance ghost. . . . The brother of the wife rebuked the woman, and the husband's people blamed him for cruelty towards his wife. Both man and wife admitted their faults and asked for forgiveness. . . . The wife's curse posed a permanent threat for husbands with a tendency to trouble their wives. Everyone knew that if a man persisted in troubling his wife she might commit *kir*. It operated as a break in situations when relationships between husband and wife steadily deteriorated, mainly due to the man's fault. But it also offered an opportunity for a settlement of serious problems by a solemn ceremony. (p'Bitek 1971, 147–48)

p'Bitek talks about the "fierce vengeance ghost" as a potential risk of the wife committing suicide, showing how the injustice suffered by the wife, if not dealt with, could eventually transform itself into a collectively suffered injustice through cen. What is highly interesting in p'Bitek's passage is that he illustrates an instance of a community member's wrongful behavior as the direct effect of relational dynamics among *living* community members, in which the nonliving or spiritual beings play less of an active role. In the case of the wife committing *twacco kir*, described by p'Bitek, it is not ancestors influencing her but rather her living husband who is driving her to despair. The point is, once again, that both the postwar extreme cen and p'Bitek's mundane cen are expressions of relationality, which is the ethical grounding of ideas of responsibility and justice in the Acholi tradition.

Punishment

The historical use of punishment in traditional Acholi justice practices is complex to investigate, both because of the absence of written documents from which to retrieve a history of its use and because of the presence of a powerful narrative that maintains the use of prison sentences and the death penalty to be against Acholi values and morals.[16] This narrative was supported by many of my interlocutors. It was also disproved by many others. During my participation in the Marcus Garvey Pan Afrikan Institute student presentations on traditional justice practices in Uganda, I listened to accounts of harsh punishments that were traditionally used to discipline wrongdoers, including in Acholiland. p'Bitek, for one, provides one very detailed account of atrocious punitive measures that were used in Acholi against people suspected of witchcraft:

> When a dangerous witch was caught . . . his punishment was extremely severe. A long, dry stick was forced through his rectum to his mouth, or a long nail driven through his head, or he was given a good beating with clubs. . . . When a *la-jok* has been killed the usual ceremonies and rituals that followed the killing of a foe in battle or clansman accidentally killed were not carried out. The killer of the witch neither earned a title, *nyingi moi*, for his deeds, nor paid compensations. . . . When he [the witch] was killed, his ghost troubled nobody. (p'Bitek 1971, 125–26)[17]

In my dialogue with KKA prime minister Kenneth Oketta, he referred to the practice of being chained in the rwot's compound as a form of punishment while philosophy professor Wilfred Lajul mentioned excommunication as the worst type of punishment used in the past. Other noncorporal punishments mentioned by interlocutors were related to stigmatization and other deterrence mechanisms such as the transmission of songs recounting someone's wrongdoing, not passing the wrongdoer's name on to the following generations, or being repeatedly publicly admonished.

The narrative that denies the historical use of punishment in Acholi is often accompanied by another powerful contemporary narrative that tends to equate the restorative paradigm of Acholi jurisprudence tout court with forgiveness. The strong presence of this discourse is associated both with the Christian rhetoric of forgiveness spearheaded by the Acholi clergy (Allen 2006; 2010) and with the South African Truth and Reconciliation Commission's (TRC) paradigmatic reference to the moral concept of ubuntu as inextricably related to forgiveness, which has become associated with a pan-African ethic and jurisprudence (Allen and MacDonald, 2013).

One of the very rare African philosophical texts dedicated entirely to the question of punishment is Odera Oruka's *Punishment and Terrorism in Africa* (1985 [1976]), of which to date the most in-depth scholarly study is Oriare Nyarwath's "Ubuntu and Oruka's Humanitarian View of Punishment" (2019).

Oruka's ideas on punishment are particularly relevant for a philosophical analysis of ATJMs because of their profound engagement with notions of responsibility both from the perspective of Western moral philosophy and from what Oruka (1985 [1976], 12–13) vaguely refers to as *traditional Africa*: "In much of traditional Africa, those who stole food merely to quench their starvation or hunger were never censured or punished for their action. In fact the action was never regarded as a theft or crime. What a pity that the action is regarded as a serious crime in colonial and post-colonial Africa."

Throughout Oruka's text, his reference to traditional Africa remains vague, generic, and never substantiated with concrete examples relating to specific African societies. What is interesting for the purposes of the present analysis, though, is to understand the significance of his reference to traditional Africa as a paradigm of jurisprudential *difference*, because what lies at the heart of this difference is precisely the concept of responsibility that underlies the practice of punishment. Oruka (1985 [1976], 8) starts one of his reflections by stating that "because in conventional law and morality responsibility is defined in terms of free will and punishment or blame is justified in terms of responsibility, free will, despite its vagueness, appears to be indispensable in criminal law and morality."

It is the choice of the word *conventional* here that is so very interesting— what does Oruka mean by "conventional law and morality"? Are they *Western* law and morality? Why would these be referred to as conventional by an African philosopher? By attributing conventional significance to Western law and morality, Oruka is upholding Western law and morality as paradigmatic while also indicating that punishment and blame are a matter of convention: they make sense only within Western jurisprudence and moral theory that posit responsibility in relation to free will. They make sense, that is, according to Western traditional justice and morality but not necessarily according to Luo traditional justice and morality.

In fact, similar observations about punishment for theft are offered by historian A. B. C. Ocholla-Ayayo in his *Traditional Ideology and Ethics Among the Southern Luo* (1976, 94):

> In actual and final judgement, many facts which appear to a European judge as irrelevant to the case are considered, and may reshape the final judgement of the case. For instance I once became a witness in a case where a man was charged of having stolen food. The witnesses were effective enough to establish the validity of the charges, and the man accused and accepted that it was true that he had stolen food, but added, "I was hungry and when they saw me, they hid the food under the bed. I asked for drinking water, but not even gruel, Nyuka, which was left in the vessel, *Dag-nyuka*, could be given to me!" The case against the thief was dismissed on the ground that the accuser had also violated moral laws of hospitality. The elders argued that if the man had to die because of hunger, he could have turned into a *Jachien*, a ghost, since he had seen food, and the whole of that lineage of the man who refused him food would have suffered the consequences.

These excerpts, taken from two academic pieces written by two Kenyan (Luo) scholars, attest to the moral and jurisprudential complexities involved in judging an act of theft in the presence of hunger. Even though these accounts date back to 1976, they were echoed in present-day Acholi in relation to theft and punishment according to Acholi traditional custom: "People look down upon theft in Acholi, especially stealing from gardens. But it is also believed that if someone is on a long journey and sees a field of groundnuts and he just branches and takes enough to eat to sustain him on the road, that's not considered to be theft. So it's a very complex jurisprudence. The owner of this garden cannot come and start beating up this person. But if you park a bicycle and take a full sack of groundnuts, now that is a crime."[18]

Oruka's philosophical discussion of punishment centers on his rebuttal of conventional notions of free will, which he links to Kantian moral philosophy. Oruka (1985 [1976], 8) makes clear that without the notion of a free will, "all the actions and choices of the individual would be determined by forces outside himself and hence all of them would be *unavoidable*." Without the notion of free will, it would also be impossible to establish the legal basis of mens rea.[19] Oruka challenges the notion of will that is implied in these moral and legal norms on the basis that "it is an almost impossible task for anyone to be able to show sincerely what it is we exactly mean when we say that one was able to exercise 'free will.'"

His major contention with the Kantian principle lies in what is implied in the notion of free will, which for Oruka is not morality but rather blame or punishment. Against what he describes as Kant's vague and metaphysical notion of the will, Oruka advances two concepts of absolutely/naturally and humanly unavoidable actions: under the first the individual has neither ability nor opportunity to control or alter a certain action while under the second the individual can refrain from action only at the cost of doing serious damage to his own life or well-being or to the lives or well-being of his community. The example Oruka (1985 [1976], 13) gives is of a person who steals food "as the only possible means open to him if he is to avoid starving to death," which for Oruka amounts to an action or a crime that is "intentional but unavoidable (humanly unavoidable)." This leads him to conclude that "we may come to establish or determine that some or all of the causes or factors that induce people to commit crimes are beyond their control."

Oruka's considerations of what he calls humanly unavoidable actions powerfully echo the environmental factors described in the accounts from Acholi gathered throughout this research, despite the profoundly different nature of the wrongs being analyzed; while Oruka is discussing the example of food theft to quench hunger, the Acholi scenario is one of crimes against humanity. The point of analyzing African theories of punishment comparatively throughout time is not aimed at trivializing the gravity of the wrongs committed in Acholiland or to try to equate groundnut theft with mass slaughter and rape. Rather, the comparison is employed to investigate the way responsibility and punishment are conceptualized in Acholi and African moral and legal philosophy and to understand why the notion that individuals are to be blamed and punished in virtue of having acted on the basis of their free will is questioned in the traditional justice process, which is not so interested in attributing individual culpability and prescribing individual punishment but rather in the reestablishment of peaceful relations between conflicting parties and long-term conflict resolution.

Questions of punishment are strongly related to the element of interrelations that so deeply inform considerations of responsibility. Many of my interlocutors described punishment as extending beyond the individual to include his/her/their relations, since the individual is always situated within a wider relational universe in which the effects of punitive action affect other members of the community: "You see the Acholi believed that if I steal your chicken and you take me to courts of law and I am jailed for four months and I am a breadwinner in my family, you are even punishing a child who is still suckling, because his diet will obviously change because of my absence."[20]

This relational understanding of punishment that informs the traditional jurisprudence is something quite different from equating justice with forgiveness, a notion I did not come across once in the course of my research. While I did come across the notion of forgiveness as constituting an essential *aspect* of the Acholi justice process, this was never posited at the exclusion of retributive measures that may also feature in the same process. There seems to be a conceptual fallacy surrounding the role of forgiveness according to ATJMs, whereby what can be clearly observed as the secondary (if not marginal) role of punishment in relation to the ultimate goal of a justice process results in a translation of Acholi justice as simply tantamount to forgiveness. Okello, for one, attributes this misunderstanding to a question of cultural translation:

> Acholi forgiveness is not the same forgiveness in English. . . . When you talk about forgiveness it has to do with, "I am very sorry you forgive me." And then I say, "Okay, you are forgiven." But the Acholi forgiveness is not that—Acholi forgiveness is a court: tell us what you did. You have to tell the whole story. You have to account. After accounting, you are condemned first. You did something wrong—something beyond human belief. You are going to do ABCD. That is the compensation. You must bring a goat, you must bring this. . . . The only thing is that we are not going to kill you like the state law says but you have gone through the same thing. Paramount elders will listen, but they will not bring witnesses. They only cross-examine you. . . . They will not really cross-examine you, they will probe. For example, I will say, "It was near the river, that is where I killed," and they will say, "Where? Was there anybody?" "No there was nobody. I was alone." "Where is the body?" They will just probe, but they will not cross-examine you like [in] court.[21]

Although Acholi ideas of justice should not be read as being synonymous with forgiveness, it is nonetheless obvious that the question of punishment constitutes a central node of contention between the traditional jurisprudence and a legalistic approach to justice that has as its ultimate aim the punishment of the offender. The centrality of the punish/forgive aspect of a justice process as differentiating Western and Acholi ideas about justice is highlighted by Owinyi in his account of working with Western partner organizations during the consultation process for the promulgation of the Amnesty Act in 2000: "This is something that I find interesting when we were advocating for Amnesty Law with our sister organizations in the West: we would go together up to a certain distance. But when it came to pardoning someone who has committed a crime, then we would separate paths!"[22]

Owinyi's considerations of the Amnesty Act and the role of blanket amnesty are particularly interesting because while he validates amnesty for being a more "culturally rooted" approach, he also exposes the promotion of amnesty as a tool of last resort, more pragmatically focused on ending the conflict rather than as an expression of deeper philosophical conceptions of justice. At the same time, Owinyi also concedes that "there are people who are really genuinely yearning for peace and then there are people who are saying, 'Okay, let us just have peace and then any other issue can be sorted out later.'"[23]

Perhaps what Owinyi means here by "any other issue" is precisely the issue of justice, which has to be sacrificed in order to have to peace.

There was widespread agreement among the different interlocutors mentioned here that a justice process that is truly just should not generate more suffering in the community, such as in the example cited above where a suckling infant would suffer from a judicial deliberation. Instead, the general collectivity and all the environmental relations should be taken into account as much as possible, and ngol ma opore should reduce collective suffering as much as possible. Most described a just justice process as one that generates a win-win situation for all conflicting parties involved rather than generating judgment in favor of one party only, which would create ill feelings in the other party, thus perpetuating tensions and conflict rather than putting them to rest:

> You know the concept of justice in its legal system I think has something to do with listening to both sides of the story and then passing

judgment, whereas in the Acholi system it is not quite passing judgment, but it is giving opportunity for the two parties to open up themselves and accept to be brought together, to be reconciled. Certainly, when it comes to translating the word *justice*, it will go hand in hand with what the legal system does. It says you will arbitrate, you kind of act as an arbitrator, as somebody who brings in a final statement that satisfies both parties. That is really where the Acholi justice system kind of differs slightly. . . . It has more to do with mediation. Win-win situation. Mediation.[24]

A fundamental element to achieve justice in the terms described above is truth telling, which a strict focus on judgment could compromise. Truth telling is a fundamental aspect of the justice process both during the actual reconciliation process between the two parties and before the initiation of the process, during the initial voluntary confession of the wrongdoer to his/her/their community or clan members. It is described as a process of appeasement for all the ill feelings that are generated from wrongful acts and as a necessary step for the commencement of the actual justice process through which the wrong has to be redressed. It appears that if the aspect of truth telling were omitted from the process, no justice could be carried out.

The importance of truth telling in the justice process was made evident in the course of my research in a number of oral accounts in which the idea was expressed that if comprehensive and total truth telling does not take place, the mato oput process will either be put off or will fail to foster reconciliation. What the majority of my interlocutors voiced as one of the essential elements of the truth-telling process is the expression of true remorse on behalf of the wrongdoer(s) for the harm caused to the offended, together with sincere feelings of empathy and sympathy for the offended party's sufferings. This goes as far as to encompass the deep feelings of the offender, based on the notion that if mato oput is performed without real conviction it will not work because in the absence of honesty the harboring of bad feelings lingers on. My interlocutors all noted that guilt, remorse, a good conscience, and honesty are strictly required for an effective reconciliation process to commence and as the conditio sine qua non for the offender to seek and eventually receive forgiveness from the offended party. An elder from Payera whom I interviewed defined remorse as *cwiny cwer*, literally translatable as "leaking liver," which he explained in terms of guilt, immorality, and evil.

Okumu agreed with the use of cwer cwiny to indicate a feeling of guilt or remorse, though he separates this concept from conscience, of which cen, according to him, is the metaphoric rendering. Such emphasis placed on the individual wrongdoer's inner feelings and motives during truth telling completes the notion of responsibility according to Acholi jurisprudence, demonstrating that it is not conceptualized only in nonindividualistic terms.

Truth telling connects, in turn, to the other fundamental aspect of the process, which is the understanding of the profound causes of conflict. Almost every single one of my interlocutors maintained that the function of truth telling in a justice process is one of the major points of contention with the formal Western justice system. To many of my interlocutors, the fact that truth distortion is a legitimate aspect of a justice process—and something that a good lawyer in fact should encourage if he/she/they are to effectively help their client—is such a paradox that it cannot even be conceived of without admitting to the profound immorality of the Western justice system: "*Wazungu* [white people] do like this: they give you the Bible and you swear: 'I am Auma. I will stand in this court to tell the truth to everybody. I will do so, so, and so.' And you will start telling lies to people. And the lawyer will enter. And there is no lawyer in Acholi. Lawyers mean you are a liar. You can turn something that is good into a bad thing. That one is not good, it is not our culture."[25]

Auma's statement above is important also as a demonstration of a typical identification of positive qualities—such as truthfulness and honesty—within Acholi culture, which many associate with the Acholi past, as a normative bliss from which to retrieve moral imperatives. An example of this notion of purity associated with past ways of life can be seen in her answer to my question regarding the risk of false accusations: "That one would never happen in our culture. It is not our culture. In our historical memory there is nothing happening like that. Someone accusing you for nothing? Why? No, no, no."[26]

Ocen makes a similar point when he says that in the past Acholis were honest because "it was just in their genes, they could not lie."[27] These statements about the effectiveness of spontaneous truth telling were contradicted by other accounts that I gathered, which describe remedial measures customarily used in Acholi in case the "ingredient" of truth telling was perceived to be missing from the process. These measures included coaxing and convincing as well as coercing, sometimes even through violent or highly intimidating means. Edward and Omar, for example, said that in the past spirit mediums were oftentimes consulted in cases where the whole truth was believed to have been concealed, though they emphasized that presently the referral to supernatural forces is done only in extreme cases when the normal procedures are not followed. In legal terminology, these are described as instances of "trial by ordeal," embodying the negative concept and practice of "justice by persuasion."[28]

While it is obvious that lying is prone to occur in *any* justice system and *any* society—including the Acholi one, as is demonstrated by the recurrence of coercive measures of truth telling just described—and that most human institutions are, in fact, vulnerable to abuse and to manipulation, these obvious considerations should not elude the important conceptual dimension of the issue voiced by Auma—namely that in her eyes, lying constitutes an *inherent* element of the Western justice system rather than its abuse. She associates lying with the figure of the lawyer who is meant to get his/her/their client acquitted even if this means bending the truth to the court, which for her is simply incompatible with justice.

Virtually every one of my interlocutors described the ultimate aim of the Acholi justice process as restoration. According to Okumu (2009, 12), restoration is achieved through the two reconciliatory principles of Acholi justice mechanisms: "reconciling an Acholi individual with his or her own conscience," a process that, according to Okumu, is furthered through nyonno tonggweno, and "reconciling an individual to another individual or group of persons" through tumu kir and mato oput, respectively. Interestingly, Okumu's description of internal reconciliation calls to mind the Socratic notion of conscience as "the two-in-one," whereby the individual is conceptualized as an interiorly relational being. This idea was echoed by a young Acholi researcher who said that the aim of the Acholi justice process is to reconcile the offender with himself/herself/themselves, with the community, and with the ancestors.[29]

Relationality is reconciliation's ontological grounding, which, according to Okumu, governs the African idea of justice as the maintenance of "good relations" among all of the existent:

> Now when you come to the Acholi people I tend to buy what Tempels and the others say: it is not a priori principles, but it is relational. It remains relational—the presupposition is: this exists, this exists, this exists—what is the link? What is the interlink? That becomes the

African preoccupation. The African thinking. What is the interlink? How can all this be together? And especially, it becomes very preoccupying because it must be a good interrelation. So, the question then becomes about the harmonious relations. How harmoniously can these be retained together? This becomes priority number one.[30]

The ethical expression of this relational ontology pertains to the harmonious interrelations of the existent, and the prerogative of justice is reconciling the variety of life's expressions.

Most of the accounts I gathered in Acholi placed the restoration of the perpetrator as a central aspect of the justice process without questioning its viability and without expressing reservations as to whether all wrongdoers *can* in fact be restored. The only strongly dissenting voice on this subject was Ochola's, according to whom certain acts are so beyond the human realm that they in fact challenge the very humanity of the one who commits them, becoming conceptualized not as crimes by human beings but rather as crimes by Obibi, the ogre. Ochola (2014, 16) maintains that in the past, the commission of such acts disqualified the perpetrator from the possibility of undergoing a restorative justice process because "one who indulged in them was in the realm of demons; and there was no *Mato Oput* with Obibi!" An example of such a demonic act, according to Ochola, is rape:

> Rape was only done by the ogre, the Obibi, what we call Obibi is ogre. Obibi would do rape. But the ultimate punishment for that was death; there was no forgiveness for it because it was done by somebody who was not a human being, because ogre was not a human being, but a human being was not expected to do things like that. So, if somebody did something like that, he became an ogre. Not a human being. But if a human being killed another human being, it means that that person, woman or man, has actually lost his or her humanity. You are no longer human being.[31]

Ochola's account seems to divide people into two categories: those who temporarily lose their humanity—and can therefore aim at having it restored through a justice process—and those who have ceased to be humans because of the nature of their acts, which excludes them from the possibility of reconciling through mato oput. Ochola's notion that traditionally what were conceived of as "inhuman acts" were not restored through a justice process but were simply suppressed is particularly interesting in light of the dominant discourses that deny the traditional use of the death penalty in Acholiland.

Porter advances a very interesting interpretation of Obibi by relating it to the Acholi folktale "Min Ayaa" ("Mother of Ayaa"). In this tale, an ogre rapes Min Ayaa. The ogre is then defeated by one of Min Ayaa's sons, called Lightning, who strikes him several times until he dies, which leads Porter to conclude: "Obibi's death posed no threat to social harmony. In fact, killing him was required to restore it. Because the crimes committed by Obibi are so dark, and so counter to Acholi values and the foundations of social harmony, that recognizing their existence as attributable to merely human causes in itself might threaten the possibilities of restoring social harmony" (Porter 2013, 275).

The function of Obibi seems to be that of impeding the admission of a type of wrongdoing that is so severe it can be neither restored nor healed. In the post northern war context, many (if not most) of the crimes committed by LRA combatants were precisely of that "inhuman" kind attributed to Obibi. And yet Ochola, who so openly spoke about the unreconcilable nature of Obibi's crimes, was also one of the strongest advocates for the use of restorative justice mechanisms with LRA combatants. This is despite the fact that his life and the lives of his loved ones were so gravely impacted by LRA crimes, as can be read in this testimony:

> Like so many families in Northern Uganda, I have also become a victim-survivor of the LRA insurgency. Our first daughter, [the] late Joyce Adong Ocola, died under mysterious circumstances on May 1, 1987, in Gulu. Winifred and I were still in North America at that time, too far away to be of help to our daughter. She was forcefully picked from our house in Gulu by some rebels who gang-raped her. She was so traumatized that she committed suicide. Ten years later in 1997, my dear wife, [the] late Winifred Ocola, was blown to pieces by a landmine allegedly planted by LRA rebels. She died instantly. I felt like a tree split by lightning from top to bottom. Her tragic death became one of the hardest challenges in my life. But I decided to dedicate my whole life to work for peace so other people do not suffer unjustly. (Ochola 2014, 29)

Personhood

The figure of Obibi calls into question major philosophical debates regarding concepts of personhood in African ethics and moral theory.

According to a major trend in African moral philosophy—one of the most known exponents of which is Nigerian philosopher Ifeanyi Menkiti—personhood is attained progressively in a dynamic relationship between the individual and the community. In line with Menkiti's (2004, 172) idea that "personhood is something which has to be achieved, and it is not given simply because one is born of human seed," South African philosopher Mogobe Ramose has also theorized ubuntu philosophy in similar terms.[32] Ramose's (1999, 52) rendering of the Nguni Bantu precept of ubuntu is that "to be a human being is to affirm one's humanity by recognising the humanity of others and establishing humane relationships with them." What this means is that "be-ing human is not enough. One is enjoined, yes, commanded as it were, to actually become a human being." As explained by Graness (2019, 153), interdependence and interconnectedness are considered the main features of Ubuntu philosophy, referring not only to the relationship between people "but also to the relationship between human beings and the entire universe."

Daniel Komakech's (2012, 140) account of "human being" in Acholi (*dano*) falls perfectly in line with the normative conceptions of personhood within African philosophy:

> The Acholi concept of *dano* (human being) is not only an ontological being as presence (an opposite of absence) in a biological way but, characteristically, *dano* is heavily founded on character, behaviour and conduct. As a result, an Acholi would cry out that "you are not a human being," not because you have suddenly changed into a cabbage but that your character, behaviour and conduct do not indicate any human being in you. That means, the concept *dano* is deeper and reaches rather to the very reality of what makes you a human being, namely, humanness. . . . *Dano* philosophy focuses on humanity and humaneness for the purpose of constantly building a social harmony. *Dano* is therefore understood as good social or communal co-existence and being each other's keeper and neighbour. In this respect, one who kills, for example, loses humanness, and the Acholi would refer to him as *pe dano* (not a human being).

Philosopher Bernard Matolino (2011, 34) has highlighted the risk of such normative views of personhood where humanity/humanness risk becoming an attribute that can be denied to some on the basis that they do not possess the ontological traits that make them human, such as babies, or "those who fail in their adulthood to acquire the epistemological tools to inform and guide their moral actions" and for this reason "are considered to be worse, ineffective, or to have completely failed at personhood."

From a different yet related perspective, a strong critique to the deployment of humanity as a normative concept in the Western liberal culture comes from Sam Dubal's (2018) ethnographic research among former LRA fighters. Dubal writes that the ICC arrest warrants of LRA combatants for crimes against humanity contributed to removing the perpetrators from humanity's sphere of belonging (37). Dubal's claim is that "it is primarily through a *modern* moral rubric that violence and humanity bifurcate" (48) producing a liberal, hegemonic concept of humanity that attempts to "monopolize control over compassion, justice and the moral good" (12). Dubal critiques the Acholi concept of humanity (*dano*) for "responding to specific demands that the discourse of humanity puts on them" (25), which Dubal believes are steeped in colonial, Western paradigms.

While I personally do not think that African normative conceptions of humanity such as those of ubuntu philosophy are all linked to Western discourses/demands and they are steeped in their own cultural traditions, I see the importance of Dubal's critique of humanity/ humanness/ubuntu when employed as normative orientations that can end up being used to oppress, usurp, and marginalize. These normative approaches are, however, rarely encompassing of an entire cultural tradition, and are rather the expressions of a certain interpretation of the cultural tradition, for which alternative interpretations always exist *within* the very same tradition. My point is that the choice between competing interpretations within the same cultural tradition is a *political* matter rather than a cultural one. The choice is between progressive and conservative philosophies of justice, and these different approaches exist within all cultural traditions. Philosophical interpretations of the tradition are vital in helping to discern between the two.

Together with the important concerns regarding normative ideas of humanity and personhood, another important concern to raise regarding Komakech's (2012, 134) conception of *dano* is the description of the "Acholi moral order" as God-mandated and enforced through the political structure of the chiefs and elders in what could be classified as a quasi-theocracy, with the rwot placed immediately after the ancestors in the ontological as "the overall administrator of the people, [who] carries out the policies that God, ancestors and the people command and want respectively."

Despite the fact that Komakech also emphasizes that Acholi cosmology is not rigid and reactionary, and that the ontological hierarchy is dynamic and renovating, his overall presentation of the ontological hierarchies that humans must conform to appears to be in sharp contrast to any notion of dynamism (2012, 134–35): "Each and every being (especially humans) knows his or her specialized tasks and ought to perform them. Failure to live up to expectation results in a rebuke, punishment or the wrath of God falling on oneself, family, clan and even the society. . . . Actions that contribute to the stability and dynamics of this order are judged morally good, while those that created instability are seen as morally bad."

A similar description of an Acholi quasi-theocratic order is offered by Latigo, who writes that prior to the British colonial administration, the Acholi traditional government was

> rooted firmly in their religious beliefs, norms and customs, which demanded peace and stability in Acholiland at all times, based on their philosophy of life. . . . In this society, traditional religion was the source of the principles of governance. The *rwodi*, or chiefs, who headed the Acholi traditional government, were believed to have been chosen by the supernatural powers. . . . They worked or governed strictly through the intercession of 'masters of ceremonies' or an aide-de-camp known as the *luted-jok* and under the guidance of the most powerful Council of Clan elders, called the *Ludito kaka*. . . . As the governing body, the Councils of Elders at all levels dealt firmly with recalcitrant individuals and groups and ensured that everyone conformed strictly to the Acholi world view. (2008, 102–03)

In these accounts, the traditional polity is taken as a paradigm of adherence to traditional cosmologies, where the role of community members is to stick to their specific position in the political hierarchy, which is directly derived from the ontological hierarchy. The moral order of Acholi society is described as strictly dictated by religious codes to which only male leaders—such as the chiefs and elders—have access.

Cameroonian philosopher Fabien Eboussi-Boulaga (1959) has in fact labeled these approaches in African philosophy "ontologically deterministic." The term comes from his critique of certain schools of thought in African philosophy that followed in the steps of Belgian missionary Father Temples's *Bantu Philosophy*. Boulaga's critique of Temples's book is summarized by Masolo (1994) as a text whereby Bantu philosophy is none other than the *negation* of the normative sphere of the Bantus. This is because, in Temples's depiction, the Bantu moral universe is posited as uncritically derived from a cosmological order that is to be unquestionably conformed to. Further, such order remains static over time so that what is deemed morally right in Bantu society is simply the perpetuation of that ever-fixed order. With this cosmological principle guiding all of Bantu life, moral agency is reduced to the simple act of alignment to what is deemed the correct balance in the greater hierarchy of forces. Eboussi-Boulaga calls the moral philosophies that align with these ideas ontologically deterministic because they deny Africans their human responsibility by simply deriving ethical and legal conduct from African cosmologies. In terms of morality, ontological determinism "is oppressive and does not give room for freedom of action" (Masolo 1994, 153). In terms of jurisprudence, deriving the legal order from the same cosmology leaves very little space for disquisition to determine the fairness of specific judicial deliberations.

Among contemporary Acholi intellectuals, there are many who uphold ontologically deterministic views or philosophies. For the most part these are either members of the clergy or devout practicing Christians. Komakech's description of the Acholi belief system undoubtedly presents striking similarities to what both Tempels and Mbiti define as the ontological hierarchy of beings according to African religions: "The Acholi distinguish *Rubanga* (God), who is above all; below him we have the *Kwaro* (the first fathers of the Acholi); *Jo muto* (the living dead); *Rwot* (Chief); *Ludito* (elders); *Coo* (men); *Mon* (women); *Lutino* (children) and the least forces like *Lee* (animals), *Yadi* (plants) and *Jammi ma pe kwo* (inanimate beings)" (Komakech 2012, 134).

Like Tempels, Komakech upholds the notion of vital force as the basis of this ontological hierarchy, where Rubanga features as "the highest being or force," "Creator," "Almighty God," "All-knowing," "Lord of all time and space," "The Absolute reality, the origin of all that was, is and will be; the Absolute ground, the Sole and the explanation of the universe" (Komakech 2012, 134).

According to such descriptions, moral order—a central aspect of which is the precept of reconciliation—is based on religious order. Further, moral action is identified with the *command* of a higher being (i.e., the Acholi god): "Each of [the five social and political levels of Acholi society] has different principles of organization but there is one principle that cuts across all. It is the theological and consequently the moral principle. . . . The moral command to reconcile comes from the Acholi god, *jok*, who lives among the Acholi people in the sacred shrines" (Okumu 2009b, 13)

According to Okumu, justice practices are thus religious acts "of profound acknowledgment of the spiritual existence of a human person created by a Supreme Being" (Okumu 2009a, 9) so that the social, political, and moral realms are inextricably linked to the religious one: "The consequences of the disputes and infightings were not only detrimental to the Acholi social and political systems, but constituted an insult to the Acholi deity, *jok*, who always wished the Acholi to live harmoniously with one another in unending happiness" (Ibid., 10).

Most of these thinkers' syncretistic religious approaches uphold the existence of both the Christian God as creator and moral arbiter of the universe *and* the Acholi traditional deities and values. The majority of them also ultimately reconnect the Acholi deities and spirits to some notion of a supreme being. This is attested to in Ochieng's notion of a bigger jok called Lubanga, under which smaller joggi operate and even interfere:

> The big *Jok* is called Lubanga actually. But in between you have so many *joggi* between *Jok* and the human beings. The *joggi* are the small gods, each clan among the Luo has its own *jok*—like if you go to Pajule you will have Lagoro, you go to Payera here you will have Kalawinya. . . . You have the *joggi* in the environment, just in the wilderness there are so many *joggi*—in the rivers, so many *joggi*; in the mountains, so many *joggi*, in big trees so may *joggi*. If you have not offended them, they will not attack you.[33]

Another example is Okumu's distinction between chiefdom joggi and the highest god, *jok-kene*:

Jok-kene is not some deity who lives up there and has nothing to do with the lives of the people. *Jok* lives concretely in the heads of families, grandparents, chiefs and ancestors all of which are somehow gods, *jogi*. They are not however *jogi* in the pantheistic sense. . . . Each of the 52 known Acholi chiefdoms has its *jogi* highest of who is *jok-kene*. For example, today the people of P'Oranga have Olal-teng, the people of Pa-Ayira have Kalawinya, Pa-Jule have Lagoro, Kock have Lokka and so forth. These are chiefdom gods and are in no way equal to *jok-kene*. (Okumu 2009b, 14–15)

The existence of a supreme being in Acholi belief systems is one of the major points of contention in p'Bitek's *Religion of the Central Luo*, where he fervently maintains that the idea of a "high god" among the Central Luo was a construction of Christian missionaries' proselytizing efforts in the region from the beginning of the twentieth century; in their quest for a local word to translate the Christian idea of God as "supreme being," the missionaries urged the local population to "elect one of the *jok* to the position of creator" (1971, 45), eventually coming up with jok Rubanga (also written as Lubanga).[34] Against British anthropologist Evans-Pritchard's notion that *Juok* among the Anuak is an all-powerful and omnipresent spirit and against Godfrey Lienhardt's idea that the Shilluk *Juok* was one in essence, p'Bitek (1970, 71) instead maintains that "there is no evidence to show that they [the Nilotes] regard the named *jogi* as refractions, or manifestations, or hypostases of a so-called High God. Each category of *jok* is independent of other *jogi*, although some are used against others. For the Nilotes there are many deities. Not one."

For p'Bitek (1970) this is clearly reflected in the fact that "the Nilotes do not speak of *jok* without adding the 'proper name' or specifying clearly the category and also the particular *Jok* they have in mind" (70) and do not indicate *Jok* as "some vague power they communicate with" (71). p'Bitek's position that a "supreme being" was never venerated among the Acholi is also upheld by Wright (1940), who argues that the concept of force among the Acholi—often associated with abnormal manifestations of power personified through different joggi—was mistaken by missionary priests for the worship of a deity. According to p'Bitek (1970; 1971), the term *jok* was traditionally used to refer to particular chiefdom deities (such as Jok Baka of the Patiko chiefdom or Jok Lokka of the Koc chiefdom); to ancestors who were invoked with their particular names;

to hostile spirits who caused diseases (such as Jok Odude or Jok Kulu); to the harmful power of witches, referred to by name (such as Jok of La-Pyem); and to deities coming from afar, who were referred to with the names of the countries from which they came (such as Jok from Madi). Joggi were represented through both material and nonmaterial forms, and they could also be known through the senses;[35] they were objects of ritual activities that could promote the well-being of the community or individual and combat ill health but also cause misfortune. Most chiefdom joggi were endowed with some human attributes and resided in remote places like forests, hills, mountains, or rivers where their shrines were built and tended by priests (p'Bitek 1970; 1971).

p'Bitek (1971) writes that the most important religious ceremony in Acholi traditions was the annual feast at the chiefdom shrines, over which the priests presided and during which the ghosts of the clan ancestors would be invoked to protect the living members of the clan; hostile spirits that caused ill health were asked to leave, since most misfortunes were interpreted in terms of jok. These were seen as cast by free joggi (who cast misfortunes or threats onto the entire chiefdom); ancestors (who visited the living with illnesses if they were neglected); or diseases that bore the names of free joggi. Traditionally, the role of the ajwaka (spirit medium) was precisely to identify the particular jok responsible for ill health or ill luck. p'Bitek (1971) provides a detailed account of the types of possession that were traditionally experienced in Acholi and divides them according to possession by ancestral spirits, by clan joggi, and by other free joggi, which can be either friendly or unfriendly and were dealt with through specific procedures led by an ajwaka).

p'Bitek (1971, 82) also highlights the separate spheres of influence between the chiefs and the priests in the course of the annual feast, where the chiefs would withdraw from the scene, becoming private persons in the village of the priest and thus losing their normal chiefly prerogatives so as to not detract from "the preside and status of the priest."

This attitude of the chiefs ensured that the annual chiefdom jok feast was a time for spiritual rather than political matters, though p'Bitek (1971, 83) ultimately concludes that in fact the annual feast had "important political and social implications but little religious consequences." This is because the ancestors who were seen as more intimately concerned with the living were the lineage ancestors, to whom prayers were addressed more regularly at the clan shrines (abila or kac). The chiefdom jok was seen as more removed from the lives of the individual clan members and was not expected to deliver much assistance in return for people's sacrifices. This leads p'Bitek (1971, 82) to a conclusion about the more political nature of the annual feast—that it was aimed at uniting the members of the chiefdom through sacrifices and prayers for the benefit of all. Most importantly, it brought about the settlement of conflicts between persons and groups because "cleanness of heart" was required to attend the feast. These aims were guaranteed precisely through the political neutrality of the priests, for they "were not directly involved in the inter-clan and inter-lineage feuds and quarrels that had to be settled before the annual feasts."

p'Bitek's research into Acholi religion and beliefs contradicts the findings of one of the most influential theorists of African religions, Kenyan Anglican priest and scholar John S. Mbiti. In his book *African Religions and Philosophy*, Mbiti (1969, 29) maintains that people in all the three hundred African societies outside the traditionally Christian and Muslim communities in which he conducted his research, "without a single exception . . . have a notion of God as the Supreme Being" and that "this is the most minimal and fundamental idea about God, found in all African societies." Among African names for God that Mbiti lists in a subsequent book entitled *Concepts of God in Africa* (1970), there is also Jok (or *Juok'* or *Juong*) from Sudan and Uganda (Mbiti 1975, 45). Mbiti describes African ontology as generally constituted by five categories:

1. *God* as the ultimate explanation of the genesis and substance of both man and things.
2. *Spirits* being made up of superhuman beings and the spirits of men who died a long time ago.
3. *Man* including human beings who are alive and those about to be born.
4. *Animals and plants*, or the remainder of biological life.
5. *Phenomena and objects without biological life*. (Mbiti 1969, 15–16)

His hierarchy of beings is strongly reminiscent of Placide Tempels's work, which deeply influenced the early theological studies of African religions conducted mainly by Christian missionaries or African converts to Christianity, many of whom have been criticized for producing agenda-driven research with the aim of demonstrating similarities between African religions and Christianity to facilitate conversions.[36]

According to the ontologically deterministic interpretations, an idea of justice emerges that is dictated strictly by religious codes to which mainly the Acholi leaders (most of whom were male elders) had full access and to which the other members of the community adhered so as not to break with custom; however, these should not be taken as the *only* philosophy of justice that arises in the interpretation of ATJMs. What I hope emerges from my own analysis of the dialogues conducted in Acholi is a very different concept of justice: one that is open, inclusive, and determined by specific situations in context, presenting a high level of public participation to moral life and norm setting in line with what Cameroonian philosopher Jean Godefroy Bidima defines as *palabre* (palaver). Palabre for Bidima (2014, 16) is the "space" where traditionally African society "interrogates its reference points, looks at itself from a distance, and can enter into uninterrupted dialogue with itself and other" so that "in Africa, one encounters palabra at every level of civil society since words give rise to meaning on every occasion." These interpretations of the tradition as geared toward palabre are more vested in whether Acholi cultural traditions can help the Acholi find justice in the aftermath of what they suffered, rather than in the rigid hierarchies of the traditional order, and they emerge more powerfully in oral conversations with local sages than in written essays by academics and members of the clergy.

What is clear from the many and varied philosophical interpretations of Acholi justice practices gathered in this chapter is that Acholi traditional justice is an open concept that lends itself to both conservative and progressive applications, both of which emerge in the postwar context, both being mobilized differently for different political ends. My overall argument is that however diverse the interpretations may be, the attributions of responsibility that have been analyzed in this chapter need to be understood as conceptually informing Acholi philosophies of justice—and not merely as mechanisms of psychosocial healing or as avenues toward peace at the expense of justice. It is only their proper guise of ideas of justice that they can enter the arena of *political philosophy* and be analyzed comparatively with other ideas of and approaches to justice.

4 The Justice Question

The Risks of Collective Guilt

In the Western tradition of moral thought and jurisprudence, the question of collective responsibility has raised and continues to raise hugely controversial debates that have been importantly influenced by one of the West's major theaters of crimes against humanity: the genocide of the European Jews, known as the Holocaust or Shoah, carried out principally by the German Nazi government.[1]

One very interesting philosophical debate on the question of collective guilt in the post-Holocaust European context can be read in the Royal Institute of Philosophy journal, in a series of articles titled "Collective Responsibility" written in 1948, 1968, and 1969. In the 1948 article, H. D. Lewis cites the German case when turning over the question of collective guilt in scenarios of mass violence and collective suffering. Lewis (1948, 15), a strong supporter of individual liability, asserts that when "war guilt" is involved, much more wisdom and patience are required to understand the dynamics of "men in the mass." However, Lewis worries that in such times there is the risk of turning to non-Western moral philosophies, which he derogatorily calls "barbarous" and "primitive" and which, in his opinion, provide reason enough for discrediting them.[2] Lewis thus openly associates processes of collective responsivity with a "primitive" way of thinking that is thus not apt for a respectable justice process, emphatically maintaining that "no one is morally guilty except in relation to some conduct which he himself considered to be wrong" (15) and that "no one can be responsible, in the properly ethical sense, for the conduct of another. Responsibility belongs essentially to the individual . . . but if the difficulties do amount to be insurmountable . . . then the proper procedure will be, not to revert to the barbarous notion of collective or group responsibility, but to give up altogether the view that we are accountable in any distinctively moral sense" (3).

Lewis thus concludes that it is preferable to give up the idea of moral responsibility altogether in contexts of mass crimes rather than to explore concepts of collective wrongdoing and collective responsibility. While Lewis (1948, 12) does concede that instances of collectivization of responsibility and guilt may sometimes be required for diplomatic and political reasons—to make peace between warring nations or to maintain civic peace, for example—he strongly maintains that any profound and meaningful attribution of moral responsibility can be attached only to an individual agent: "To accept responsibility for others for practical purposes, to incur certain consequences for what another has done, is one thing; to be morally accountable is another; and in this last regard we cannot answer for one another or share each other's guilt (or merit), for that would imply that we could become directly worse (or better) persons morally by what others select to do—and that seems plainly preposterous."

Lewis thus completely downplays the environmental and societal dimensions that impact individual agents and maintains that moral accountability is a strictly individual matter. In an example very similar to the one used by Oruka, which was discussed in the previous chapter, Lewis (1948, 13) also cites the case of theft of food by someone who is hungry—in Lewis's example it is a poor woman who steals a loaf of bread to feed her children—only to reach a conclusion that is diametrically opposed Oruka's: "'A structure' cannot be the bearer of moral responsibility; neither can 'society in general,' for these are both abstractions which we must be careful not to hypostatize. . . . The guilt of the poor woman is lessened, if not eliminated altogether, by her circumstances. But she alone is to blame, if blame there is to be, for what she herself has done."

The debate initiated by Lewis in this issue of *Philosophy* was picked up again twenty years later in the very same journal by D. E. Cooper and R. S. Downie. Cooper's (1968) article argues in favor of certain instances of collective responsibility in cases where wrong or fault cannot be analyzed in terms of individual liability. He thus shows the limits of theories of individual responsibility in certain contexts and challenges their universal validity. Downie refutes Cooper's point by insisting that while collectives can be held causally or legally responsible, it is impossible to ascribe any *moral* responsibility to collective entities. For both Lewis and Downie the question is really one of *moral responsibility*, which they think can be ascribed only to individuals. Though Downie

(1969, 68) also makes a sociological concession in terms of the complexity of dealing with the dynamics of "role-acceptance" that may influence individual members of a collective in a certain direction, he nonetheless maintains that "the decision to act as a member of a collective is basically an individual decision which carrie[s] moral responsibility with it."

What is striking about this debate is how passionately the individualists Lewis and Downie argue for the impossibility of collective responsibility on moral grounds. This example of a Western philosophical moral debate is clearly not representative of the entirety of Western moral philosophy, not all of which has centered the individual as the exclusive agent of moral thought, action, and duty. It is important to mention here the philosophical ethics of Emmanuel Levinas (1969), centered on the idea of an encounter with the Other that does not reduce or incorporate the Other into the self. Another important name is that of Paul Ricoeur; a philosopher who is working within the Western tradition and very attentive to the question of nonindividual responsibility.[3]

But if one must single out a thinker from the Western philosophical tradition who has most carefully and passionately vivisected questions of individual and collective responsibility—and has done so in the aftermath of mass atrocities—that is Hannah Arendt.

Hannah Arendt was particularly preoccupied with the pitfalls of collectivization of guilt in the aftermath of the Holocaust. She worried that a nonlegalistic approach to the question of responsibility incurred the risk of creating a scenario wherein everyone is held morally responsible and no one is held criminally accountable; to put it in more simply, where everyone is guilty, no one is guilty. In her famous book *Eichmann in Jerusalem: A Report on the Banality of Evil*, Arendt ([1963] 1977, 5) unequivocally states that "justice demands that the accused be prosecuted, defended, and judged, and that all other questions of seemingly greater import—of 'How could it happen?' and 'Why did it happen?,' of 'Why the Jews?' and 'Why the Germans?,' of 'What was the role of other nations?' and 'What was the extent of co-responsibility on the side of the Allies?' of 'How could the Jews through their own leaders cooperate in their own destruction?' and 'Why did they go to their death like lambs to the slaughter?'—be left in abeyance."

The meting out of *legal* justice was essential for Arendt in countering what she perceived as a general trend in her time to shy away from judgment by shifting responsibility to "the bigger picture," be it the system, an ideology, or history itself. Against these ideas that tended to shift the question of accountability to an abstract and collective level, Arendt (2003, 29) maintained the principle that "there is no such thing as collective guilt or collective innocence; guilt and innocence make sense only if applied to individuals" and that "morally speaking, it is as wrong to feel guilty without having done anything specific as it is to feel free of all guilt if one is actually guilty of something" (28).

In the Acholi context, concerns with regard to the pitfalls of collective guilt have been raised importantly by Adam Branch (2011). Branch in particular warns against the risks of an interiorization of guilt on behalf of the entire Acholi population, which an uncritical application of ATJMs may lead to, and which ultimately elides the appropriate political response to what was in fact a civil conflict: a balanced apportionment of responsibility on both sides—the GoU and the LRA. Branch is thus wary of community conflict resolution mechanisms that can end up teaching communities in crisis to define violence "among themselves as the full extent of the violence they face, to blame themselves for the violence, and to see the solution to violence and to conflict as residing in their won embraces of less violent and less conflictual activities and attitudes" (131–32).

What joins Arendt's and Branch's critiques to the risks of collective responsibility is that these are not moved by a contempt toward moral philosophies centered around collectivities but rather by a profound respect for the sufferers of mass violence, both in their collective and individual dimensions. A response that can perhaps be advanced to their critiques is that while caution should be exercised toward ideas and processes of collective responsibility because they may inhibit virtuous justice processes by preventing accountability for wrongs committed and end up creating narratives of self-blame, perhaps the same caution should be raised against the risks of excessively individualizing all forms of responsibility. The risk of excessive individualization is that the bigger picture of the conflict gets lost and the real causes of collective suffering are left unexplored, making it impossible for them to be addressed.

This is a risk that in fact pervades Arendt's writings. Despite her strong support for the criminal prosecution of Nazi criminals as a right step in the direction of justice, her writings leave the reader with a sense of unsatisfaction as to the way responsibility for the horrors of the Holocaust was morally and socially addressed in post–World War II Europe. What remains a point of great interest and curiosity when engaging with Arendt's work on collective responsibility is that despite her strong stance against facile collectivizations of guilt, Arendt remained profoundly unsatisfied and concerned with the types of sociocultural and sociopolitical considerations that arose out of the experience of Nazism in Europe. Though she vehemently argued that certain types of questions "should be left in abeyance" ([1963] 1977, 5) by the courts of law when trying to establish liability for the mass suffering caused by Nazi crimes, these are precisely the types of questions that so deeply concerned her as a moral and political philosopher. Much of her work—especially her collection of essays posthumously grouped under the title *Responsibility and Judgment* (2003) by Jerome Kohn—is pervaded by the questions "how could it happen?" and "why did it happen?" for she felt that unsatisfactory answers at the moral and cultural levels would come to constitute one of the greatest predicaments in European history: the Old Continent would never be rid of Nazism as an ideological and political possibility that could always make a comeback. This unsatisfaction is precisely in relation to the question of collective responsibility for the perpetuation of mass crimes against civilians under Fascism and Nazism, in which so many citizens participated either directly or indirectly or simply did not denounce as wrong and did not try to prevent in any way.

Instead, ATJMs are enabled to explore the real causes of conflict because they are equipped with measures to address the collective and social dimensions of responsibility that characterize theaters of collective suffering. Community-based collective responsibility provides a holistic view of the wrong committed by an individual community member, one that tries to look at all possible environmental factors that influence the individual as a member of a collective entity. The aim of the Acholi justice process is the *survival* of both the individual wrongdoer and his/her/their community. This survival is ensured by placing individual liability, blame, responsibility, and guilt in an environmental context by way of moral philosophies that connect the individual and his/her/their actions to other beings. These moral philosophies tend to reduce individual culpability in favor of community-based collective responsibility so that the business of righting wrongs becomes a community prerogative in an effort to move forward.

The Risks of Ethnojustice

The second most important critique that has been directed at contemporary uses of ATJMs in the aftermath of the war is that it is a form of ethnojustice, once again by Adam Branch. Drawing on Hountondji's (1983) critique of ethnophilosophy to denote a similar phenomenon in the study of non-Western traditions of justice, Adam Branch (2011, 163) defines ethnojustice as a discourse reserved for non-Western cultures that blends elements of ethnography, law, and morality to describe traditional justice systems. It falls into the same predicament as ethnophilosophy by purporting to describe "a single, coherent, positive system that is presented as being universally, consensually, and spontaneously adhered to by all members of that culture, and that, even if in abeyance today, remains valid and should be revived."

According to Branch, the ethnojustice discourse in the Acholi context draws on past institutions to inform present-day decision-making in a manner that gives rise to a picture of Acholi culture that differs from the image of inclusivity and participation it claims to be reviving. Branch (2011, 167) finds that in its efforts to revive a romanticized Acholi past of "spontaneous, universal and consensual adherence to spiritual dictates for the good of the Acholi as a whole," ethnojustice in fact propagates the "enforcement of a certain set of norms, couched in a spiritual language, by male elders and others claiming the mantle of chiefship who claim the exclusive access to that spiritual domain in order to ensure the reproduction of their preferred social order."

Branch (2011, 164) further maintains that ethnojustice has been largely promoted by foreign NGOs operating in northern Uganda in their endeavor to establish that "traditional justice is just as genuine a system of justice as western justice" that "meets the requirements of western justice and human rights," thus presenting Acholi traditional justice as "a local articulation of universal standards of justice and human rights." Tim Allen (2006; 2010) also largely attributes the systematization and codification of Acholi practices to foreign agents (such as development partners and NGOs) working in the region and preoccupied with securing funding for their activities. Allen's (2010, 251) skepticism of such types of codification stems from his own experience living in Acholi and Madi villages in the 1980s, where he found that "it was rare for rituals to be given special names" so that when "someone was asked what a particular ritual was called they were likely to find the question a bit strange. The answer was usually a straightforward description of what has happened." This leads Allen (2010) to conclude that if there ever were a system of traditional justice—in the sense of a standard range of rules and regulations for dealing with offenses that was applied beyond the immediate moral community of neighboring lineages—it was to a large extent the product of British indirect administration. According to Allen (2006, 132), "the current consensus about customary Acholi conceptions of justice" has emerged largely from traditional and religious leaders in Acholi—mainly the Council of Elders Peace Committee, the Council of Chiefs, and the Acholi Religious Leaders Peace Initiative (ARLPI), all of which are concentrated in Gulu—and the international aid agencies that fund them.

Mahmood Mamdani's critique of the role of tradition in current African political and legal discourse is also key to understanding the ethnojustice critique. Mamdani ([1996] 2017) has strongly critiqued the judicial hybrid that arose under the system of indirect rule—applied throughout British-occupied Africa—which applied customary law in the colonies by seizing and re-creating local customs and traditions as a way for the colonial state to govern the territory efficiently. Under this system, the affairs of "the natives" were placed under the control of the Native Authority, an administrative body headed by Europeans but enforced on the ground through local chiefs. These chiefs were appointed directly by the colonial government and were in no way coherent with the customary political structures that the indirect-rule philosophy claimed to maintain. According to Mamdani's analysis, the colonial government's unlimited political support of these local chiefs in return for their keeping order among natives—through tax collection and the application of highly punitive measures for all those who challenged the government—gave rise to new political figures whose power became increasingly despotic and arbitrary.

The notion of customary law that arose out of the colonial experience "consolidated the non-customary power of colonial chiefs" and "came to enforce as customs rules and regulations that were hardly customary" (Mamdani [1996] 2017, 122). The system of indirect rule thus created a situation whereby the law served as an instrument of demarcation between citizens and subjects and where the latter came to be governed by brute force under the flag of customs in the exclusive grasp of the chief, who featured as "the petty legislator, administrator, judge and policeman all in one" (54). This political system of decentralized despotism is, according to Mamdani, the "hallmark of the colonial state in Africa" (39), which was so efficiently propagated through the salvaging of "the widespread and time-honoured practice . . . of a decentralised exercise of power" and by freeing that power completely of the "restraint of peers and people" (Ibid.) that had characterized most precolonial African polities, whether monarchical or not. It was a form of political rule aimed at the entrenchment of colonial interests but made to pass as being in line with the customary values of the colonized. This system is also described by Murungi (2004, 521) as the "Euro-Western jurisprudence of colonialism" whereby "Indigenous African tribunals, 'chiefs,' 'kings,' 'leaders,' and councils of elders were used to facilitate the subjection of Africans to a Euro-Western jurisprudential regime."

There is, however, another aspect of tradition that Mamdani also importantly raises: the emancipatory potential of tradition. Mamdani ([1996] 2017, 183) refers to this as the phenomenon of "modern tribalism," which has come to embody the "form of rule" of the colonial state but which also may become "the form of revolt against it" where "the former is oppressive [while] the latter *may be* emancipatory." Tribalism, according to Mamdani, has historically been treated as either a primordial residue of premodern Africa or the result of a modern conspiracy. This means that tribalism is seen as either a tool employed by outside forces interested in dividing and ruling or a tool embraced from within by local elites interested in gaining advantages for themselves—a reading that clearly emerges from many of the critiques of ATJMs that are reviewed in this chapter. What interests me instead is the other more neglected dimension of modern tribalism that Mamdani alludes to: tribalism as a political avenue of self-affirmation and political emancipation of a collectivity.

Throughout my fieldwork I repeatedly came face to face with the existential, political, social, and psychological need to affirm the Acholi identity across the Acholi population. Most of my interlocutors showed palpable anxiety—though it was undoubtedly much more pronounced among the elders—when they described how the war had destroyed a people, a land, a culture, a tradition; that the youth no longer knew what it meant to be Acholi; and that the transmission of oral traditions that used to be passed on from one generation to the next were interrupted by the brutality and degradation of camp life. This is a form of anxiety that understandably would emerge among survivors of mass violence since it is their group identity and existence that have been targeted. It is in fact the same type of anxiety that Hannah Arendt (2007, 42) points to in "The Jewish Question" when she writes:

> After the catastrophe of 1933, the slogan heard in all Jewish camps was: *teshuva*, repentance, return to Judaism, let us take stock of ourselves. . . . The collapse of 1933—which was a political, economic, and ideological collapse and at the same time the collapse of an entire spiritual world, including its values and what turned out to be only seemingly safe possessions—has led not to a new flourishing of Jewish life but to apathy and, in terms of the young, to a kind of rebarbarization. . . . The slogan of "return" is an admission of one's own guilt, both politically and, if you will, morally. This is already expressed in the word *teshuva,* or taking stock of oneself.

Arendt here is linking the teshuva with survival and is showing how there is a line connecting the admission of guilt and attempts to regenerate a broken community that is otherwise prone toward falling into "barbarization" as an effect of what it suffered. The fact that in the Acholi case this call is led by the elders should not be interpreted only as their attempt to secure power and privilege within their communities but also as their attempt at leadership and at wanting to steer their communities in a direction of spiritual and material reconstruction rather than watching them fall into abandonment and despair.[4]

This call of taking stock of oneself redirects us to another political thinker, the already cited Antonio Gramsci, who writes in *Selections from The Prison Notebooks* (1999, 628) that "the starting point of critical elaboration is the consciousness of what one really is, and is 'knowing thyself' as a product of the historical process to date which has deposited in you an infinity of traces, without leaving an inventory. The first thing to do is to make such an inventory."

The importance of making an inventory and reconstituting the community is particularly important in the context of mass violence toward select ethnic or minority groups and especially in contexts where legal redress is hindered, leaving the affected communities to make sense of the violence and loss suffered on their own in an overall vacuum of governance, law and accountability.

I believe that the crucial point is *how* such inventory is conducted because the *how* is what constitutes the discriminating factor between a retrogressive versus a progressive use of tradition (or tribalism), as elucidated by Mamdani ([1996] 2017, 24): "It is not enough simply to separate tribal power organized from above from tribal revolt waged from below so that we may denounce the former and embrace the latter. The revolt from below needs to be problematized, for it carries the seeds of its own fragmentation and possible self-destruction."

Reading the question of collective responsibility in terms of the two possible uses of modern tribalism—oppressive v. emancipatory, retrogressive v. progressive—I would argue that ATJMs' emancipatory potential lies precisely in not conflating collective responsibility with collective guilt. This conflation is avoided through the truth-seeking mechanism of ATJMs, which ensures that individual perpetrators are in fact brought forward in the justice process and thus clearly differentiated from nonperpetrators. In this sense, maintaining the traditional ritual elements of Acholi justice process can help against political instrumentalizations of the conflict, which always hinge on attributions of guilt. Opposite of the political instrumentalizations of collective responsibility is instead a political justice approach that is not aimed at distributing collective guilt at the expense of individual accountability, but rather is aimed at political reform.

Collective Responsibility as Political Justice?

Mamdani (2015; 2015; 2020) holds that the criminal justice paradigm, which centers on individual prosecution and treats violence as a criminal act, cannot provide the political reform that is so urgently needed in contexts where populations have survived mass atrocities.

The problem with the criminal justice paradigm is that it does not distinguish between different *scales* of violence and judges specific singular acts of violence indiscriminately in contexts of both small-scale and mass violence. In so doing, it fails to distinguish between different *types* of violence: political violence, which is issue driven and requires supporters that make up its political constituency, and criminal violence that really just needs perpetrators. For this reason, Mamdani advocates for political justice, as this is the type of justice needed to deal with the legacies of political violence. Political justice is focused on political reform and on the future survival of groups and is particularly apt in contexts of mass violence because it provides an analytical tool for understanding that violence (Mamdani 2020; 2015). This approach also works well in contexts where the victims of mass atrocities have to carry on living side by side with their perpetrators, as is clearly the case in Acholiland and in most of the conflicts afflicting the African continent.

Mamdani's argument is that without an understanding of the causes of mass violence—which a criminal justice approach is not meant to provide, as it is beyond its aims and scope—that same violence will continue in new forms. A criminal justice approach, which is centered on individual accountability for criminal acts, cannot address the political aspect that is always entailed in mass violence, and for this reason Mamdani criticizes the ICC model of international criminal accountability as unsatisfactory.

Mamdani illustrates these two different approaches to justice via two emblematic historical processes of dealing with crimes against humanity on a mass scale: the 1945–46 Nuremberg trials of top Nazi offenders, led by the Allied forces who defeated Germany in World War II, and the negotiations that ended apartheid in South African known as the Convention for a Democratic South Africa (CODESA). Mamdani (2015, 158) states, "Whereas Nuremberg shaped a notion of justice as criminal justice, CODESA calls on us to think of justice as primarily political. Whereas Nuremberg has become the basis for a notion of *victim's justice*—as a complement rather than an alternative to *victor's justice*—CODESA provides the basis for an alternative notion of justice, which I call *survivor's justice*. CODESA shed the zero-sum logic of criminal justice in favour of the inclusive nature of political justice."

Mamdani proceeds to argue that the CODESA paradigm is much more relevant to the resolution of civil wars in Africa, as it allows for a contextual understanding of violence as a political phenomenon that has to find a political solution.

With regard to the conflict between the government of Uganda and the LRA, Mamdani interestingly argues that the moment of political justice was the passing of the Amnesty Act by Parliament in 2000. However, he concludes that this process—which could have served as an important prelude to the LRA's participation in a political process— was eventually undercut by President Museveni's appeal to the ICC in 2005 that ultimately "sabotaged both the democratic process within the country and the overall peace process" (Mamdani 2015, 192).

Mamdani describes the resolution of the northern Uganda conflict as oscillating between political justice and criminal justice approaches, eventually landing in favor of the latter. This oscillation reflects the constantly changing dynamics of the conflict, characterized by moments of governmental negotiations/concessions with the LRA and moments of refusal to compromise with the LRA, attempting military solutions instead. If the first peace talks of 1995, the Amnesty Act of 2000, and even the Juba peace talks of 2006–08 can be read as signals toward political justice—intended as willingness to negotiate peace among all warring parties—the frequent military operations, the state referral to the ICC, and the creation of the ICD signal instead toward a criminal justice approach and a one-sided narrative of the historical causes of mass violence in Uganda.

Branch (2016, 48) has pointed out the strategic agenda that underlies this oscillation, whereby the Ugandan government uses the ICC to endorse its innocence, guaranteed by the ICC's "myopic focus on prosecuting the LRA alone." As discussed already, the ICC's partisan prosecution with regard to the northern Uganda conflict has been highlighted as one of the greatest hinderances to a fair and inclusive justice process. Many Acholi interlocutors I engaged with during my research felt that ATJMs would help to provide a much truer picture of the conflict than what would emerge in both national and international courts of law. According to an Acholi scholar, this is a crucial point in understanding one of the most widespread criticisms of the ICC in Acholi, which is that the court focuses only on LRA crimes while ignoring the atrocities committed by the government and the UPDF:

> That is where the Acholis have a problem with the ICC and the government. The ICC wants to say the government is innocent and Joseph Kony and his team are completely guilty. But the Acholi people say, "No! We know how many atrocities were committed by the government forces, we know how many atrocities were committed by Joseph Kony. We know all of them bear some responsibility. We know probably Joseph Kony's responsibility outweighs that of the government but that does not make the government totally innocent." So when you come with a direct justice system where one is innocent, the other one is guilty, the Acholi will not understand because they know that it is never one person alone who is 100 percent guilty. In most cases guilt lies on both sides in case of conflict,

and when guilt lies on both sides the only difference lies in degrees. And that is why most justice systems among the Acholi are remedial in nature but not punitive. It is remedial in the sense that they want to restore a damaged relationship. They want to put back the distrust that was created out of sin. And that is where true justice comes when an offense committed has been paid for. Remunerated. Guilt has first been acknowledged so first there is acknowledgment of guilt. In the traditional Acholi context, that is the moment of truths—not truth. Truths is the total openness.[5]

Amid all of the polarized, unilinear, and one-sided accounts of the mass violence committed in Acholi, the traditional justice paradigm tries to make its own truths by continuously referring to the contextual, collective, and political dimensions of that violence. What can appear as a troubling expression of self-blame that is entailed in the Acholi collectively taking on Kony's bal ujebu can also be read as a restorative attempt to collectively own responsibility for the confusion, frustration, and loss that was clearly felt by the large part of Acholi society that Kony catalyzed. According to such an approach, Kony is absolved for being an expression of a moment in time in Acholi history, the sacrificial catalyst of a widespread political crisis, and his doings and wrongs are owned collectively.

To try to provide a conclusive thought on whether ATJMs can be used as an avenue to pursue political justice, I believe that the answer can be positive only if ATJMs are viewed in relation to the wider national justice process. Currently, the National Transitional Justice Policy (NTJP) states that the government has undertaken development, recovery, and peace efforts in some parts of the country through development programs "in a bid to make good for post conflict communities in various parts of the country" (Republic of Uganda, NTJP, 2019, 12). However, the policy also highlights that "nevertheless, the challenges pertaining to reparations still persist. This has created anger, frustration, resentment, and psychological challenges in post conflict communities [which include]: i) the absence of a comprehensive Government policy to address reparations needs of communities affected by conflict" (12–13).

It seems to me that the real challenge of pursuing justice in Acholi does not lie primarily with the cultural tradition of the jurisprudence of choice—Western versus African, traditional versus modern, Indigenous versus international—but rather with the political climate in which justice is being pursued. In this climate it is extremely difficult to conduct balanced prosecutions given that one of the parties to the conflict—namely, the Ugandan government—remained in power after the war, and it is not clear whether it intends to feature as a party to the national transitional justice process and to what extent. This was highlighted by many scholars and activists working in Uganda at the time of my research as the challenge of pursuing transitional justice in a context of no regime change. In this climate both the traditional Indigenous African and the modern criminal Western responses to justice will inevitably become politically instrumentalized, as I found to be the main concern of the Ugandan intellectuals and activists working in the field of traditional/Indigenous justice that I dialogued with in the course of my research. Their preoccupation was seldom that Ugandans could be shortchanged of justice proper because the traditional justice mechanisms were not up to standard but rather that traditional justice mechanisms would be instrumentalized by the state in a manner that would serve selective justice purposes. Professor Luutu expressed this in terms of the state being a "night dancer" that on one side acts the part of having come to its senses by responding to dissatisfied communities' complaints with the kind of justice delivered by the state (hence the call for and inclusion of traditional justice mechanisms as part of the national transitional justice agenda) while on the other side it purports that traditional justice lacks legitimacy (on the counts of discrimination, conformity with international human rights standards, uniformity, and predictability).[6] The state assumes the role of bringing traditional justice mechanisms "up to standard," thereby gaining total power and control over processes that are by definition centered on high degrees of local autonomy and public ownership. Luutu thus warned against the formalization of traditional justice mechanisms in a manner that deprives them of true "jurisprudential parity," thus perpetuating the colonial legacy of customary law that continued well after independence, with many African governments simply further institutionalizing existing Western systems by replacing the dual colonial system with one that either abolished customary law or "integrated them into the bottom rung of the judicial ladder" (Robins 2009 40).[7]

The risk of using traditional justice is that they end up being instrumentalized for a specific situation that is transitory in nature and

that serves select political ends, thus clearly defying the quest for jurisprudential parity advocated by intellectuals and activists such as Luutu.
This critique resonates with critiques of legal pluralism in legal scholarship, which Griffiths (1986, 7), for example, condemns for being "a fix-
ture of the colonial experience and one of the most enduring legacies of
European expansion" and "a messy compromise which the ideology of
legal centralism feels itself obliged to make with recalcitrant social reality." The defective aspect of this compromise, according to Griffiths, is
enshrined in the Hegelian notion of progress whereby "allowances must
be made" (Ibid.) on the road to modernization and nation building. The
Hegelian aspect lies precisely in the overarching ideology that Griffiths
sees as entrenched in the merely apparent openness of legal pluralism,
where difference is not thought of as the final aim but rather as a stop
on the road to unification, which remains the eventual goal. This system thus does not treat other legal traditions from the point of parity
but rather as something that has to eventually evolve and die out, thus
revealing legal pluralism as "but one of the forms in which the ideology
of legal centralism can manifest itself" (8).[8]

Attributing a transitional function to Indigenous justice mechanisms can thus result in their furthered debasement in the overall
project of state centralization. This is precisely the critique that South
African philosopher Mogobe Ramose directs against the postapartheid
South African government's use of the moral norm of ubuntu, which
was employed in the Interim Constitution (1993) and in the Promotion
of National Unity and Reconciliation Act (1995) to sponsor reconciliation through the Truth and Reconciliation Commission (TRC) but was
eventually discarded from the final South African Constitution (1996).[9]
Though the Ugandan transitional justice scenario was not linked to
a transition in political power such as in the South African case, this
fact in itself does not diminish the risk of co-option of traditional justice mechanisms by the state to further its political ends, which speaks
to Ramose's notion that by continuing to frame African traditions of
justice as "customary law," "the right of conquest is still ruling, even
epistemologically."[10]

Failure to meet different individuals' particular demands for justice is a shared shortcoming of both the modern/democratic/formal and
the traditional/tribal/Indigenous systems. That is because the actual application of liberal democracy—*especially* in its postcolonial form—is

inevitably studded with its own pockets of oppression, which is true of almost any political system, whether it be traditional African, modern European / North American, or contemporary African. The conclusion as to which political system has proven to be more or less oppressive to the Acholi people is extremely difficult to draw given the complex history of the region. Von Benda-Beckmann (1984, 31) elucidates the abuses of power that are prone to mar the so-called democratic justice institutions when he writes, "There are at least as many bureaucrats and chiefs who further their own economic and political positions through 'created' Western law as there are African village heads doing so through the application of 'traditional law.'" For him this ultimately results in a scenario where "distortions may be much worse than those which the customary law suffers when falling into the minds of Westernized lawyers and bureaucrats."

My own critique as to whether the formulation of ATJMs in the aftermath of the war qualify as instances of political justice relates more to the manner in which they address the bigger picture of responsibility or not. The important political process initiated by Acholi civil society in demanding that the legacies of war be addressed in a way that focuses on Acholi survivors and how they would come to reconstitute a community that has been harmed and displaced for twenty years risks falling short of political justice proper if it circumscribes the responsibility for the mass violence that occurred in Acholiland as only within the bounds of the Acholi community, thus hindering what Mamdani (2015, 9) defines as a prerequisite for a truly political justice process: "a double acknowledgement by both sides to the conflict." Whether this will be achieved and in what terms—perhaps under the aegis of the new National Transitional Justice Policy—remains to be seen in the next phase of Ugandan political history.

Conclusion

THE TENSION BETWEEN the Acholi ethnic identity and their national identity as Ugandans is the red thread that runs throughout this book, for it is the tension that shaped the northern Ugandan war and that continues to shape the quest for justice in the aftermath of the war. The troubled political identity of the Acholi, oscillating between the traditional polity and the colonial and postcolonial state, characterized the northern Ugandan war as being in fact two wars in one: an intra-Acholi civil conflict between LRA supporters and Acholi civilians and a civil war between the LRA and the government. This double level of conflict importantly informs the question of justice that followed the war, with Acholi traditional justice processes highlighting the many ways in which the atrocities committed in the course of the northern war were the product of the collective unfreedom and of the limited political agency suffered by the Acholi in their contemporary history.

I believe that the use of ATJMs as described in this book does in fact provide a viable path toward political justice with regard to the intra-Acholi dimension of the conflict. That is because by centering community-based collective responsibility in justice processes, ATJMs enable a justice process that is inclusive and focused on the survivors of conflict. By not differentiating responsibility in terms of the causes and effects of conflict, and by framing responsibility instead as the expression of collective suffering (through jok, cen, and abila), Acholi jurisprudence is an example of survivor's justice.

The book has also showed, however, that there are different interpretations of the community-based collective responsibility principle, which give rise to very different philosophies of justice in Acholi. I have framed these into two main philosophical orientations labeled "ontological determinism" (drawing on Eboussi-Boulaga) and "palaver" (drawing on Bidima). What the existence of these diverging orientations and philosophies of justice attest to, is that ATJMs—like all justice mechanisms—are not neutral and that it is the interpretation given to them that can turn them either into a tool of oppression wielded by a minority male elite for the gain of a small dominion or into a tool of political emancipation embraced dynamically and flexibly by a collectivity that has suffered mass violence.

The potential for ATJMs to be conservative or progressive, oppressive or emancipatory, does not lie in the traditional practices per se but rather in their interpretation and use throughout time, as well as in their ability to maintain the traditional jurisprudence in conversation with contemporary emancipatory goals that necessarily exceed the traditional polity and engage the Ugandan state and the wider world. Only in this way will tradition avoid the risk of parochialism and insularity, maintaining itself instead in a dialogical, dynamic relation with all that surrounds a specific cultural community—if, of course, the community gets a chance to.

With regard to the second dimension of the conflict—which is the civil war with the government—I believe the principles of community-based collective responsibility as exposed in chapter 3 of this book do not yet qualify as instances of political justice. Unlike some of the critics of ATJMs surveyed in this book, I do not think that this is because ATJMs were traditionally used to mediate small-scale conflicts among the Acholi only and that the ideas of justice that they embody cannot be extended beyond the reach of the traditional Acholi polity. My sense is that all jurisprudences can be adapted and expanded to new and changing contexts and that Acholi jurisprudence is no exception to the rule. Even though the ideas of justice contained in ATJMs may have originated within the limited confines of the social, moral, and political universe of the Acholi clans, there is nothing in them that inherently prevents them from being applied to other contexts as they deal with the fundamental challenge of righting wrongs, something human beings everywhere in the world experience. This expansion would almost certainly entail new and different rituals or adaptations of the traditional rituals; it would also require the inclusion of new and different beings among the traditional Acholi ones in order to express new and different types of wrongdoing and suffering. Even though these adaptations are complex, my sense is that there is no inherent impediment to enlarging the principles contained in ATJMs. Further, I believe that the ideas of justice contained in Acholi jurisprudence are universally intelligible and applicable because they potentially speak to *any* situation of injustice.

My reason for concluding that the community-based collective responsibility principle—as it was explained and interpreted in the course of my dialogues—falls short of political justice is that it focuses almost exclusively on the intra-Acholi dimension of the conflict. Again, this is not due to a limitation of the principle itself, which could clearly be applied to the other party to the conflict as well, but rather to the way it has been interpreted and applied after the war. For ATJMs to meet the requirements of political justice, they would have to be applied in a manner that accounts for all the different levels of responsibility by all the parties to the conflict. The hope is that this process will be facilitated under Uganda's new National Transitional Justice Policy (2019) and that this policy translates into a platform for a fully-fledged political justice process.

Glossary

Acholi	English
Ajwaka (pl. *ajwaki*)	spirit medium
Abila	ancestral shrine
Bal	abomination (lit. "breaking")
Cen	vengeance ghost
Culo kwor (also *cullo kwor*)	compensation payment (lit. "to pay life")
Cwinyi	liver
Cwinyi cwer	leaking liver
Dano	human being
Gommo tong	bending of spears
Jok (pl. *joggi*)	deity/spirit
Kal	royal lineage
Kaka	clan/lineage
Kir	taboo/curse
Kwaro (pl. *kwari*)	ancestors
Ladit (pl. *ludito*)	elder/s
Ladit kaka (pl. *ludito kaka*)	lineage elder/leader
Lakwena (pl. *lukwena*)	another term for *ladit kaka*
Mato oput	drinking the bitter root
Mit-ot	hut mother (female head of a household)
Nebi	prophet
Ngol	to cut
Ngol ma opore	to cut straight
Ngol ma atir/ngol matir	to cut well/beautifully
Ongon	traditions, legal norms, and old precedents
Piny	surroundings
Rwot (plural *rwodi*)	chief/lord/king

Tipu (also spelled *tibu*)	spirit
Tumu kir	cleansing a taboo
Ujebu (also spelled *ujabu*)	sin
Wangoo	common fireplace
Won-wa	male head of a household

Notes

Introduction

1. While the LRA boycotted the signing of the Final Peace Agreement (FPA) scheduled to take place in November 2008, the government of Uganda on several occasions reaffirmed its commitment to implementing all other agreed-on agenda items, which included the Cessation of Hostilities (CoH) signed on August 26, 2006; the Comprehensive Solutions signed on May 2, 2007; and the Agreement on Accountability and Reconciliation, signed on June 29, 2007. In February 2007, annexes to Agenda Items Two and Three were negotiated together with a permanent ceasefire and the final agenda item on Disarmament, Demobilization, and Reintegration (DDR) (Atkinson 2010b).

2. Abductees were subjected to violent and degrading treatment, forced into combat and/or to serve as porters; many female captives were forced into sexual slavery and/or forced marriages and pregnancies (Carlson and Mazurana 2010). Among the most commonly reported atrocities that the abductees were made to commit while in LRA captivity were ritual killings of new members, killings of immediate family members, and massacres of children who attempted to escape the LRA ranks. Young adolescents were especially targeted for abduction, mainly because of their high numbers and because they were more effective guerrillas than younger children and "more easily indoctrinated and disoriented than young adults" (Blattman and Annan 2010, 381). According to the UNHCR, "At the conflict's peak in 2005, there were 1.84 million IDPs living in 251 camps across 11 districts of northern Uganda" (https://www.unhcr.org/news/briefing/2012/1/4f06e2a79 /unhcr-closes-chapter-ugandas-internally-displaced-people.html, accessed May 24, 2021). The estimated deaths in the camps calculated by the World Health Organization (WHO) in 2005 were one thousand per week.

3. The complex underlying causes of the war are discussed in chapter 2.

4. The ICC is a permanent independent court based in the Hague that tries persons accused of the most serious crimes of international concern—namely, genocide, crimes against humanity, and war crimes. The court was established by the Rome Statute, adopted on July 17, 1998, by 120 states and entered into force on July 1, 2002 after ratification by 60 countries. Situations can be referred to the court either through a state party to the Rome Statute (this includes self-referral, like in the case of Uganda), the UN Security Council or an investigation proprio motu of the Office of the Prosecutor (Schabas 2010). Of the five indicted LRA commanders, only Dominic Ongwen has been tried and sentenced to twenty-five

years of imprisonment on account of sixty-one crimes comprising crimes against humanity and war crimes, committed in northern Uganda between July 1, 2002 and December 31, 2005. Raska Lukwiya and Okot Odhiambo have been confirmed dead and proceedings against them have been terminated while Josef Kony and Vincent Otti remain at large (www.icc-cpi.int/uganda and www.icc-cpi.int /uganda/ongwen, accessed January 31, 2025).

5. The annexure was signed on February 19, 2008 and sets out a framework for implementing the agreement. JLOS is a sector-wide approach created by the GoU in 2006 that brought together institutions with closely linked mandates of administering justice and maintaining law and order and human rights.

6. The government declared the majority of IDPs free to move out of the camps in 2006. Unfortunately, I have not been able to identify accurate data regarding the exact number of ex-combatant Acholi returnees. The JLOS NTJP puts the total number of ex-combatants in Uganda who applied for amnesty at twenty-seven thousand (NTJP 2019), and a 2015 IRIN report states that at the time at least thirteen thousand were confirmed ex-LRA combatants. The NTJP also states that seven thousand returnees reintegrated into their communities, but no further information is given as to who these seven thousand were, where they reintegrated, and what happened to the other twenty thousand who were amnestied.

7. For an in-depth overview of the field on transitional justice, refer to the work of Ruti Teitel (2000; 2008). While there exists a certain degree of consensus on the mechanisms and tools that constitute transitional justice processes, there is still widespread disagreement regarding the conceptual framing of the field and the manner in which justice is defined and pursued under transitional justice policy and legislation. Huyse (2008), for example, identifies four instrumental objectives of all transitional justice policies as reconciliation, accountability, truth telling, and restitution with the objective of healing victims, repairing the social fabric, and protecting the peace; Fletcher, Weinstein, and Rowan (2009) speak of transitional justice mechanisms as trials, truth commissions, vetting, reparations, memorialization, and institutional change; Clark (2009) identifies six key themes of transitional justice in reconciliation, peace, justice, healing, forgiveness, and truth; and Sriram (2009) includes truth commissions, domestic trials, international and hybrid tribunals, and traditional justice mechanisms under the transitional justice umbrella. Doubts concerning its proper placement in the temple of justice address the unorthodox and nonlegal measures that constitute transitional justice mechanisms (such as truth commissions, apologies, and paths toward social and individual healing), question the kind of justice that transitional justice mechanisms are in fact delivering, and contend the primacy of the strictly legalistic paradigm versus other fundamental aspects of transitional justice, and vice versa.

8. Among the humanitarian literature, some of the most import reports are *The Bending of Spears* (1997); *The Hidden War, The Forgotten People* (2003) and *Roco Wat I Acholi* (2005). One excellent book that thoroughly lists and describes

a wide variety of Acholi healing and peace rituals is *Traditional Ways of Coping in Acholi* by Harlacher et. al (2006), which can also be grouped under humanitarian literature as its publication followed a community request to the Psychosocial Support Program of the faith-based organization Caritas of the Gulu Archdiocese to promote healing and facilitate reintegration. As for the academic literature on the topic, a number of studies have been produced mostly in the areas of anthropology, such as those by Heike Behrend (1999), Tim Allen (1991), Erin Baines (2007; 2010), Svenker Finnström (2008), and Holly Porter (2017), who also adds an important gender perspective; and politics and law, such as those by Chris Dolan (2009), Adam Branch (2011), Tim Allen (2006) and Allen and Vlassenroot (2010) and Phil Clark (2018). See the bibliography for full references.

9. A broader comparative analysis is unfortunately not available to me due to my lack of in-depth expertise in other philosophical traditions; my comparative readings remain inscribed within Western and African philosophical traditions.

10. I choose to refer to these as beings rather than concepts because of the Western-laden notion of concept as an abstract idea devoid of material existence. The first written definitions of jok can be traced back to Italian Comboni missionary Pasquale Crazzolara's (1938, 41) first Acholi grammar guide and dictionary, where he defines jok as "spirit (god)." Atkinson (2010a, xix) translates jok as "important god or spirit" while Behrend (1999) defines jok as a spirit, force, or power. Allen (1991, 382) defines jok as "a general term for the supernatural" and, in accordance with p'Bitek (1970; 1971), maintains that jok could also be used to denote "ancestral ghosts," mostly known as *kwari* in Acholi (singular *kwaro*). Allen further distinguishes between ghosts referred to as jok/joggi or kwaro/kwari and spirits referred to as *tipu* (sometimes also spelled *tibu*); the current connotation of tipu as disembodied spirits appears to come from Christianity whereas traditionally tipu's literal meaning, "shadow," was used to refer to the spirits of the ancestral shrine (*kac* or *abila*) (Allen 1991). Harlacher et al. (2006, 44) maintain that "*Jok* is a general term that can be translated as 'spirit force,' 'spirit power' or 'god.' A clan or chiefdom *jok*, however, was a spirit that belonged to a particular clan or chiefdom, and was typically tied to a particular place."

1. Methodological Considerations

1. Wilfred Lajul and Benedetta Lanfranchi, "Acholi Philosophy in Their Culture and Ways of Life," paper presented at the Council for Research in Values and Philosophy conference "Culture and Philosophy as Ways of Life in Times of Global Change," Athens, Greece, August 3, 2013.

2. Dialogue with Oola, September 9, 2013, Gulu.

3. Dialogue with youth, November 18, 2013, Gulu.

4. Dialogue with elder from Paico, September 13, 2013, Gulu.

5. Dialogue with legal expert, Ministry of Justice, February 1, 2013, Kampala.

6. Dialogue with human rights lawyer, February 1, 2013, Kampala.
7. Dialogue with legal expert, Ministry of Justice, February 1, 2013, Kampala.
8. Dialogue with two elders from Payera, March 24, 2013, Gulu.
9. Dialogue with Oola, September 9, 2013.
10. Dialogue with Ochieng, September 5, 2013, Gulu.
11. Odoch Pido, email to author, March 25, 2014.
12. D. A. Masolo, email to author, March 26, 2014.

2. The Context

1. The *kaka* is a fundamental social unit in the Acholi socio-political structure and importantly informs the nature of conflict resolution practices. It can
be defined as "the patrilineal clan or lineage that made up the core of a fenced
village" (email correspondence with Professor Ronald Atkinson, July 28, 2014).
The *ladit kaka* is the head of a *kaka* and the *ludito kaka* are the various heads of
all the clans/lineages that made up the chiefdom. Evidence suggests that at least
in many chiefdoms, the group of *ludito kaka* served as some sort of council to
the *rwot*, perhaps more structured in some chiefdoms, less so in others (email
correspondence with Professor Ronald Atkinson, July 28, 2014). The *ludito kaka*
are also sometimes also referred to as *lukwena* (singular *lakwena*). Currently the
use of the term "clan" in English to indicate/translate the Acholi *kaka* is very
widespread. It was originally used by Crazzolara and British ethnologist Charles
Gabriel Seligman to refer to: "Branches of the same agnatic lineages, between
which connection is still maintained [. . .] found both in the same domain and
also in widely scattered areas of Acholiland and even outside it" (quoted in
Girling 1960, 65). While most scholarly accounts of Acholi society employ terms
such as "agnatic lineage" or "patrilineal lineage" to translate *kaka*, the majority
of the interlocutors cited in this book use the terms "clan," "society," and "community" to refer to Acholi social and political structures, from the *kaka* level to
Acholiland as a whole.

2. The ladit kaka was the head of a kaka and the ludito kaka are the various
heads of all the clans/lineages that made up the chiefdom. Evidence suggests that
at least in many chiefdoms, the group of ludito kaka served as some sort of council
to the rwot, perhaps more structured in some chiefdoms and less so in others
(email correspondence with Professor Ronald Atkinson, July 28, 2014). The ludito
kaka are also sometimes also referred to as *lukwena* (singular *lakwena*).

3. Behrend (1999, 15) also references such balance: "The power of the *rwot* was
constantly questioned and made the object of negotiations and public discussion.
Disputes between the chief, who claimed political power, and the elders of the clan
lineage, who tried to assert their own power against that of the chief, were endemic
in Acholi; depending on the respective constellation of power in a chiefdom at a

particular time, the chief or the elders might prevail, i.e. centralist of decentralist tendencies might be realized."

4. The Catholic presence in Acholi has been particularly significant. In the course of my fieldwork, I came to learn of the also significant presence of Italians in the region through Catholic missions. A number of the earliest written accounts on Acholi culture and philosophy are in fact in Italian.

5. On May 21, 2013, the sector brought together religious and traditional leaders along with representatives from JLOS institutions, civil society, academia, and the press in an effort to build consensus on the proposed draft of a national transitional justice policy. I attended this workshop as part of the Refugee Law Project team.

6. The annexure to the agreement was signed on February 19, 2008 and sets out a framework for implementing the agreement.

7. Some of these welcoming rituals have been depicted in the film *Imani* (2010) by Ugandan director Caroline Kamya.

8. *Oput* is the name of a bitter root that grows in the region. This root is chosen for the conflict resolution ritual precisely to symbolize the element of bitterness that pervades the community following a killing.

9. In 2011, Al Jazeera released a documentary on mato oput in one of its editions of *Witness* entitled "Bitter Root." See Al Jazeera 2011, available from http://www .aljazeera.com/programmes/witness/2011/10/20111012152024670219.html.

10. This is corroborated by Girling's (1960, 67) observation that "it appears that such ceremonies were most frequently performed between villages which were part of the same domain, or which were territorially not far distant. In other cases, or where compensation, for a variety of reasons, was not offered, the blood feud operated. The agnatic kin of a dead man sought to *culo kwoo*, obtain payment, for the life of their brother, by killing his murderer, or another member of that lineage."

11. Dialogue with Rv. Fr. Dr. Joseph Okumu, February 8, 2013, Gulu.

12. Dialogue with Ochieng, September 5, 2013, Gulu.

13. Dialogues with Okello, February 6, 2013, Gulu; and with Lajul, senior lecturer in philosophy, Makerere University, April 22, 2013, Kampala.

14. Interview with Lajul, April 22, 2013, Kampala.

15. Interview with two elders from Payera, March 24, 2013, Gulu.

16. Dialogue with Oola, September 9, 2013.

17. *Ujabu* (also *ujebu)* is an Acholi term translated as "something dirty and unbecoming."

18. Dialogue with Okello, February 6, 2013, Gulu.

19. Dialogue with Rv. Fr. Dr Joseph Okumu, March 26, 2013, Gulu and dialogue with elder, September 13, 2013.

20. Dialogue with historian, September 9, 2013, Gulu.

21. Dialogue with Holly Porter, lead researcher at JSRP (London School of Economics), November 22, 2013, Gulu.

3. Community-Based Collective Responsibility

1. Dialogue with legal expert at the Ministry of Justice, February 1, 2013, Kampala. *Ubuntu* is a Nguni Bantu word that is translated as "humanity," "humanness," and "being human." It is a key concept in African moral philosophy indicating interconnectedness and relational normative ethics (Samkange and Samkange 1980; Ramose 1999; Cornell and Muvungua 2012; Ogude 2019).

2. Dialogue with Rv. Fr. Dr. Joseph Okumu, March 26, 2013, Gulu. Heraclitus is a pre-Socratic Greek philosopher who theorized the idea of the Logos, a term with which he denoted the structural order of the cosmos; the rational order of the mind (the mind's capacity to rationally discern order), and the linguistic ability to communicate thoughts to others that points to the unity underlying the apparent diversity and change (flux) present in the world (Sweet 2007).

3. Dialogue with two elders from Payera, March 24, 2013, Gulu. A term that is often used to indicate moral character in Acholi is *kwo maatir*, which literally translates to "straight life."

4. Dialogue with elder, September 11, 2013, Kitgum; and with academic, September 9, 2013, Gulu. For a detailed account of these events see Finnström 2008. See also Clark 2018, 221.

5. Dialogue with Rv. Fr. Dr. Joseph Okumu, March 26, 2013, Gulu.

6. Dialogue with Onyango Odongo, September 9, 2013, Gulu.

7. *Nebi* is a Swahili word used in the Bible to indicate a prophet.

8. Refer to chapter 2 for more information on Acholi culture, religion, and history.

9. Dialogue with Rv. Fr. Dr. Joseph Okumu, March 26, 2013, Gulu.

10. Dialogue with Rv. Fr. Dr. Joseph Okumu, March 26, 2013, Gulu. Here Okumu is referring to Kenyan theologian and philosopher John S. Mbiti, whose ideas are discussed in chapter 4.

11. Dialogue with Rv. Fr. Dr. Joseph Okumu, March 26, 2013, Gulu.

12. Dialogue with two elders from Payera, March 24, 2013, Gulu.

13. Dialogue with elder from Paico, September 13, 2013, Gulu.

14. Dialogue with Holly Porter, November 22, 2013, Gulu.

15. Dialogue with two elders from Payera, March 24, 2013, Gulu.

16. See, for example, Allen 2006; 2010. With reference to the Southern Luo, Ocholla-Ayayo (1976, 92) also maintains that corporal punishment "is not a characteristic Luo method of sanction."

17. This is a dramatically different account of the consequence of a witch's activity from the one quoted above. p'Bitek himself does not elucidate the reasons for such different reactions to what appears to be the same "crime."

18. Dialogue with Ojara, November 21, 2013, Gulu.

19. Mens rea is a legal requirement that a person is not to be held responsible for a crime unless he committed the crime intentionally, voluntarily, or with "malice aforethought"' (Oruka 1985 (1976), 9).

20. Dialogue with Owinyi, February 5, 2013, Gulu.

21. Dialogue with Okello, February 6, 201, Gulu.

22. Dialogue with Owinyi, February 5, 2013, Gulu.

23. Dialogue with Owinyi, February 5, 2013, Gulu.

24. Dialogue with two elders from Payera, March 24, 2013, Gulu.

25. Dialogue with elder, September 11, 2013, Kitgum.

26. Dialogue with Auma, September 11, 2013, Kitgum.

27. Dialogue with Ocen, September 13, 2013, Gulu.

28. Professor Mashood Baderin, Lecture on African Law, February 26, 2015, SOAS.

29. Presentation by student at the Marcus Garvey Pan Afrikan Institute, November 6, 2013, Mbale.

30. Dialogue with Rv. Fr. Dr. Joseph Okumu, March 26, 2013, Gulu.

31. Dialogue with Rt. Rev. MacBaker Ochola II, September 5, 2013, Gulu.

32. The hyphenated spelling of these terms is in accordance with Ramose's spelling.

33. Dialogue with Ochieng, September 5, 2013, Gulu.

34. This episode is described in great detail by p'Bitek (1970, 62):

> In 1911, Italian Catholic priests put before a group of Acholi elders the question "Who created you?"; and because the Luo language does not have an independent concept of create or creation, the question was rendered to mean, "Who moulded you?" But this was still meaningless, because human beings are born of their mothers. The elders told the visitors that they did not know. But, we are told that this reply was unsatisfactory, and the missionaries insisted that a satisfactory answer must be given. One of the elders remembered that, although a person may be born normally, when he is afflicted with tuberculosis of the spine, then he loses his normal figure, he gets "moulded." So he said "Rubanga is the one who moulds people." This is the name of the hostile spirit, which the Acoli believe causes the hunch or hump in the back. And, instead of exorcising these hostile spirits and sending them among pigs, the representatives of Jesus Christ began to preach that Rubanga was the Holy Father who created the Acoli."

Reference to this is also found in p'Bitek's poem *Song of Lawino*, where the Virgin Mary is called "mother of the hunchback" (1972 [1966]).

35. Not only do the *jogi* have proper names, but they can also be, as it were, known through the senses. The "soil" from the supposed original homeland is handled and carried from place to place. The rock can be seen and touched; the kites with the flames in their anuses can be seen flying through the night sky; the voices of the ghosts of the dead ancestors can be heard and identified as belonging to so-and-so; the *jok*-in-the-bundle can be bought and sold, and it makes noises like chicks, and when buried in the ground the earth around cracks. The free hostile spirits can be heard arguing with the diviner, and when captured and killed, their blood can be seen on the blade of the weapon.

This is in vivid contrast with the metaphysical aspects of Christianity with its conception of an eternal world revealed only to the intellect, but not the senses. (p'Bitek 1971, 72).

36. See, for example, Masolo 1994.

4. The Justice Question

1. Between 1939 and 1945 the Nazi regime in Germany carried out genocidal mass murders, killing around six million Jewish people and another six million non-Jewish people including Soviet POWs, ethnic Poles, Romani people, people with disabilities, gay men, and other categories of discriminated-against people (https://encyclopedia.ushmm.org/content/en/article/documenting-numbers-of -victims-of-the-holocaust-and-nazi-persecution, accessed December 19, 2023).

2. I distance myself from and strongly condemn the derogatory and offensive language used by Lewis here. The reason I am quoting it is precisely to emphasize the marginalization—if not stigmatization—of non-Western moral philosophies within philosophical debates.

3. See especially *The Just* (2003).

4. As voiced in many of my dialogues, suicide, a very painful legacy of the conflict, was being experienced across Acholi.

5. Dialogue with Acholi scholar, May 4, 2013, Kampala.

6. In Uganda, night dancers are people believed to call on the help of the dead to destroy other people during nocturnal hours. Its metaphoric use here refers to a feature of duplicity that Luutu is criticizing in the state: by day it shows one face and by night another.

7. Lecture by Babuuzibwa Mukasa Luutu, vice chancellor of the Marcus Garvey Pan-Afrikan Institute, September 2013, Mbale.

8. It is important to state here that Griffiths's criticism is with respect to a particular kind and notion of legal pluralism. Since the time of this article, the field of legal pluralism has grown immensely, producing some very positive results. For a summary of some of these see Moore 2005.

9. Presentation by Mogobe Ramose at the Council for Research in Values and Philosophy conference "Culture and Philosophy as Ways of Life in Times of Global Change," Athens, Greece, August 3, 2013; and dialogue with Mogobe Ramose, professor of philosophy at the University of South Africa, August 6, 2012, Athens, Greece.

10. Dialogue with Mogobe Ramose, professor of philosophy at the University of South Africa, August 6, 2012, Athens, Greece.

Bibliography

Al Jazeera. 2012. "Bitter Root." http://www.aljazeera.com/programmes/witness/2011/10/20111012152024670219.html

Allen, Tim. 1991. "Understanding Alice: Uganda's Holy Spirit Movement in Context." *Africa: Journal of the International African Institute* 61 (3): 370–99.

———. 2006. *Trial Justice: The International Criminal Court and the Lord's Resistance Army.* London: Zed.

———. 2010. "Bitter Roots. The 'Invention' of Acholi Traditional Justice." In *The Lord's Resistance Army: Myth and Reality*, edited by Tim Allen and Koen Vlassenroot, 242–61. London: Zed.

Allen, Tim, and Anna Macdonald. 2013. "Post-conflict Traditional Justice: A Critical Overview." JSRP paper 3.

Allen, Tim, and Koen Vlassenroot. 2010. "Introduction." In *The Lord's Resistance Army: Myth and Reality*, edited by Tim Allen and Koen Vlassenroot, 1–21. London: Zed.

Arendt, Hannah. (1963) 1977. *Eichmann in Jerusalem: A Report on the Banality of Evil.* London: Penguin.

———. 1982. *Lectures on Kant's Political Philosophy.* Chicago: University of Chicago Press.

———. 2003. *Responsibility and Judgment.* New York: Schocken.

———. 2007. *The Jewish Writings.* New York: Schocken.

Atkinson, Ronald R. 1989. "The Evolution of Ethnicity among the Acholi of Uganda: The Precolonial Phase." *Ethnohistory* 36 (1): 19–43.

———. 2010a. *The Roots of Ethinicity: The Origins of the Acholi in Uganda.* Kampala, Uganda: Fountain.

———. 2010b. "'The Realists in Juba?' An Analysis of the Juba Peace Talks." In *The Lord's Resistance Army: Myth and Reality*, edited by Tim Allen and Koen Vlassenroot. London: Zed.

Baines, Erin. 2005. *Roco Wat I Acoli. Restoring Relationships in Acholi-land: Traditional Approaches to Justice and Reintegration.* Kampala Institute for Global Studies, Gulu District Ngo Forum and Ker Kwaro Acholi.

———. 2007. "The Haunting of Alice: Local Approaches to Justice and Reconciliation in Northern Uganda." *International Journal of Transitional Justice* 1 (1): 91–114.

———. 2010. "Spirits and Social Reconstruction after Mass Violence: Rethinking Transitional Justice." *African Affairs* 109 (436): 409–30.

Blattman, Christopher, and Annan, Jeannie. 2010. "On the Nature and Causes of LRA Abduction: What the Abductees Say." In *The Lord's Resistance Army: Myth and Reality*, edited by Tim Allen and Koen Vlassenroot, 378–433. London: Zed.

Behrend, Heike. 1999. *Alice Lakwena and the Holy Spirits*. Oxford, UK: James Currey.

Bidima, Godefroy Jean. 2014. *Law and the Public Sphere in Africa: La Palabre and Other Writings*. Bloomington: Indiana University Press.

Boccassino, Renato. 1938. "La mitologia degli Acioli dell'Uganda sull'Essere Supremo, i primi tempi e la caduta dell'uomo (con testi)." *Anthropos* 33: 59–106.

———. 1962. "La vendetta del sangue praticata dagli Acioli dell'Uganda; riti e cannibalismo guerreschi." *Anthropos* 57: 357–73.

Booty, Natasha, and Swaibu Ibrahim. 2024. "Thomas Kwoyelo: Ugandan Lord's Resistance Army Rebel Commander on Trial." BBC. Last modified January 19, 2024. https://www.bbc.com/news/world-africa-68025152.

Bradfield, Paul. 2017. "Reshaping Amnesty in Uganda: The Case of Thomas Kwoyelo." *Journal of International Criminal Justice* 15 (4): 827–55.

Branch, Adam. 2010. "Exploring the Roots of LRA Violence: Political Crisis and Ethnic Politics in Acholiland." In *The Lord's Resistance Army: Myth and Reality*, edited by Tim Allen and Koen Vlassenroot, 1–21. London: Zed.

———. 2011. *Displacing Human Rights: War and Intervention in Northern Uganda*. New York: Oxford University Press USA.

Bujo, Bénézet. 1998. *The Ethical Dimension of Community: The African Model and the Dialogue between North and South*. Nairobi, Kenya: Paulines Publications Africa.

Callaghan, Sarah. 2009. *Overview of Customary Justice and Legal Pluralism in Uganda*. United States Institute for Peace, George Washington University and World Bank Conference "Customary Justice and Legal Pluralism in Post-Conflict and Fragile Societies," November 17–18, Kampala: George Washington University.

Carlson, Khristopher and Dyan Mazurana. 2010. "Accountability for Sexual and Gender Based Crimes in Northern Uganda." In *Children and Transitional Justice. Truth Telling, Accountability and Reconciliation*, edited by Sharanjeet Parmar, Miny Jane Roseman, Saudamini Siegrist, and Theo Sowa, 235–66. Harvard: UNICEF.

Clark, Phil. 2009. "Establishing a Conceptual Framework: Six Key Transitional Justice Themes." In *After Genocide: Transitional Justice, Post-Conflict Reconstruction and Reconciliation in Rwanda and Beyond*, 191–206. New York: Columbia University Press.

———. 2018. *Distant Justice: The Impact of the International Criminal Court on African Politics*. Cambridge, UK: Cambridge University Press.

Cornell, Drucilla, and Nyoko Muvungua. 2012. *Ubuntu and the Law*. New York: Fordham University Press.

Crazzolara, J. Pasquale. 1938. *A Study of the Acooli Language: Grammar and Vocabulary*. London: Oxford University Press.

———. 1950. *The Lwoo, Part I: Lwoo Migrations*. Verona, Italy: Nigrizia.

Cooper, D. E. 1968. "Collective Responsibility." *Philosophy* 43 (165): 258–68.

Cooper, D. E. 1969. "Collective Responsibility—Again." *Philosophy* 44 (168): 153–55.

Degryse, Annelies. 2011. *"Sensus Communis* as a Foundation for Men as Political Beings: Arendt's Reading of Kant's *Critique of Judgement*." *Philosophy and Social Criticism* 37 (3): 345–58.

Dolan, Chris. 2009. *Social Torture: The Case of Northern Uganda, 1986–2006*. Oxford, UK: Berghahn.

Downie, R. S. 1969. "Collective Responsibility." *Philosophy* 44 (167): 66–69.

Dubal, Sam. 2018. *Against Humanity: Lessons from the Lord's Resistance Army*. University of California Press.

Eboussi-Boulaga, Fabien. 1959. *Le Bantu Problematique*. Paris: Presénce Africaine.

Finnstrom, Svenker. 2008. *Living with Bad Surroundings: War, History and Everyday Moments in Northern Uganda*. Durham, NC: Duke University Press.

Fletcher, Laurel E., Harvey M. Weinstein, and Jamie Rowen. 2009. Context, Timing and the Dynamics of Transitional Justice: A Historical Perspective. *Human Rights Quarterly* 31: 163–220.

Fuller, Lon L. 1958. "Positivism and Fidelity to the Law: A Reply to Professor Hart." *Harvard Law Review* 71 (4): 630–72.

Gadamer, Hans-Georg. (1960) 2013. *Truth and Method*. London: Bloomsbury.

Gender against Men. 2009. Film. Refugee Law Project.

Girling, F. K. 1960. *The Acholi of Uganda*. London: H. M. Stationery Office.

Gramsci, Antonio. 1999. *Selections from The Prison Notebooks*, translated and edited by Quentin Hoare and Geoffrey Nowell Smith. London: ElecBook.

Graness, Anke. 2019a. "African Philosophy." In *The Routledge Handbook of Philosophy and Relativism*, edited by Martin Kush. London: Routledge.

———. 2019b. "Ubuntu and *Buen Vivir*": A Comparative Approach." In *Ubuntu and the Reconstitution of Community*. Bloomington: Indiana University Press, 150-175.

Graness, Anke, and Kai Kresse, eds. 1997. *Sagacious Reasoning: Henry Odera Oruka in Memoriam*. Frankfurt am Main: Peter Lang.

Government of Uganda, Justice Law and Order Sector. 2019. National Transitional Justice Policy.

Government of Uganda and the Lord's Resistance Army. 2007. "Agreement on Accountability and Reconciliation," June 29, 2007.

———. 2008. "Annexure to the Agreement on Accountability and Reconciliation," February 19, 2008.

Griffiths, John. 1986. "What Is Legal Pluralism?" *Journal of Legal Pluralism and Unofficial Law* 18 (24): 1–55.

Gyekye, Kwame. 2010. "African Ethics." In *Stanford Encyclopedia of Philosophy*, edited by Edward N. Zalta. http://plato.stanford.edu/entries/african-ethics.

Harlacher, Thomas, Francis Okot, Caroline Aloyo, Mychelle Balthazard, and Ronald Atkinson. 2006. *Traditional Ways of Coping in Acholi: Cultural Provisions for Reconciliation and Healing from War*. Kampala, Uganda: BMZ and CRS.

Hart, H. L. A. 1958. "Positivism and the Separation of Laws and Morals." *Harvard Law Review* 71 (4): 593–629.

Heidegger, Martin. (1927) 2008. *Being and Time*. New York: Harper Perennial.

Hicks, John. 2012. "Sensus Communis: On the Possibility of Dissent in Kant's 'Universal Assent.'" *Diacritics* 40 (4): 106–29.

Hiesmayr, Ella. 2022. "Found in Translation: Multilinguism and Philosophy." In *Critical Conversations in African Philosophy. Asixoxe-Let's Talk*, edited by Alena Rettová, Benedetta Lanfranchi, and Miriam Pahl. London: Routledge.

Hountondji, P. (1976) 1983. *African Philosophy: Myth and Reality*. Bloomington: Indiana University Press.

———. 1989. "Occidentalism, Elitism: Answers to Two Critiques." *Quest: Philosophical Discussions* 3 (2): 3–30.

———, ed. 1995. "Producing Knowledge in Africa Today: The Second Bashorun M. K. O. Abiola Distinguished Lecture." *African Studies Review* 38 (3): 1–10.

———, ed. 1997. *Endogenous Knowledge: Research Trails*. Oxford, UK: CODESRIA.

———. 2002. *The Struggle for Meaning: Reflections on Philosophy, Culture and Democracy in Africa*. Athens: Ohio University Press.

Human Rights and Peace Center (HURIPEC) and Liu Institute for Global Issues. 2003. *The Hidden War: The Forgotten People*. Kampala, Uganda: HURIPEC.

Huyse, Luc. 2008. "Introduction: Tradition Based Approaches in Peacemaking, Transitional Justice and Reconciliation Policies." In *Traditional Justice and Reconciliation after Violent Conflict*, edited by Luc Huyse and Mark Salter, 1–24. Learning from African Experiences. Stockholm: IDEA.

Imani. 2010. Film. Caroline Kamya.

International Criminal Court, Office of the Prosecutor. 2004. "Press Release: President of Uganda Refers Situation concerning the Lord's Resistance Army (LRA) to the ICC," January 29, 2004.

IRIN. *Forgive and Forget? Amnesty Dilemma Haunts Uganda*. Last modified June 12, 2015. https://www.refworld.org/docid/557fe4914.html.

Kant, Immanuel. (1790) 1987. *Critique of Judgment*. Indianapolis, IN: Hackett.

———. (1788) 2002. *The Critique of Practical Reason*. Indianapolis, IN: Hackett.

———. (1785) 2012. *Groundwork of the Metaphysics of Morals*. Cambridge, UK: Cambridge University Press.

Karugire, Samwiri Rubaraza. 1980. *A Political History of Uganda*. Nairobi, Kenya: Heinemann Educational.

Ker Kwaro Acholi. (s.a.). *Law to Declare the Acholi Customary Law*. Gulu, Uganda: J. B. Enterprise.

Kohn, Jerome. 2003. "Introduction." In *Responsibility and Judgement* by Hannah Arendt, vii–xxx. New York: Shocken.

Komakech, Daniel. 2012. "Reinventing and Validating the Cosmology and Ontology of Restorative Justice: Hermeneutics of the Traditional Acholi Justice System in Northern Uganda." In *African Perspectives on Tradition and Justice*, edited by Tom Bennett, 121–48. Ghent, Belgium: Intersentia.

Kresse, Kai, and Oriare Nyarwath. 2023. "Introduction." In *Rethinking Sage Philosophy: Interdisciplinary Perspectives on and beyond H. Odera Oruka*, edited by Kai Kresse and Oriare Nyarwath, 1–35. Lanham, MD: Rowman & Littlefield.

Lanfranchi, Benedetta. 2023. "'Does This Mean That There Is Philosophy in Everything?' A Comparative Reading of Henry Odera Oruka's and Antonio Gramsci's First and Second Order Philosophy." In *Rethinking Sage Philosophy*, edited by Kai Kresse and Oriare Nyarwath, 77–98. Lanham, MD: Rowman & Littlefield.

Latigo, James Ojera. 2008. "Northern Uganda: Tradition Based Practices in the Acholi Region." In *Traditional Justice and Reconciliation after Violent Conflict: Learning from African Experiences*, edited by Luc Huyse and Mark Salter, 85–122. Stockholm, Sweden: International Institute for Democracy and Electoral Assistance (IDEA).

Levinas, Emmanuel. 1969 [1961]. *Totality and Infinity: An Essay on Exteriority*, translated by Alphonso Lingis Pittsburgh: Duquesne University Press.

Lewis, H. D. 1948. "Collective Responsibility." *Philosophy* 23 (84): 3–18.

Liu Institute for Global Issues, Gulu District NGO Forum, and Ker Kwaro Acholi. 2005. *Roco Wat I Acholi. Restoring Relationships in Acholi-land: Traditional Approaches to Justice and Reintegration*. Vancouver, Canada: University of British Columbia.

Macdonald, Anna. 2019. "'Somehow this Whole Process Became So Artificial': Exploring the Transitional Justice Implementation Gap in Uganda," *International Journal of Transitional Justice* 13 (2): 225–48.

Mamdani, Mahmood. 2014. "Beyond Nuremberg: The Historical Significance of the Post Apartheid Transition in South Africa." *Politics and Society* 43 (1): 61–88.

———. 2015. "Beyond Nuremberg: The Historical Significance of the Post-Apartheid Transition in South Africa." MISR Working Paper no.23, October 2015.

———. (1996) 2017. *Citizen and Subject: Contemporary African and the Legacy of Late Colonialism*. Johannesburg, South Africa: Wits University Press.

———. 2020. *Neither Settler nor Native: The Making and Unmaking of Permanent Minorities*. Cambridge, MA: Harvard University Press.

Masolo, D. A. 1994. *African Philosophy in Search of Identity*. Bloomington: Indiana University Press.

———. 2003. "Philosophy and Indigenous Knowledge: An African Perspective." *Africa Today*, 50 (2): 21–38.

———. 2004. "Western and African Communitarianism: A Comparison." In *A Companion to African Philosophy*, edited by Kwasi Wiredu, 483–98. Oxford, UK: Blackwell.

———. 2009. "Narrative and Experience of Community as Philosophy of Culture." *Thought and Practice: A Journal of the Philosophical Association on Kenya (PAK)* 1 (1): 43–68.

———. 2010. *Self and Community in a Changing World*. Bloomington: Indiana University Press.

Matolino, Bernard. 2011. "The (Mal) Function of "it" in Ifeyani Menkiti's Normative Account of Person," *African Studies Quarterly* 2 (4): 23–37.

Mbiti, John S. 1969. *African Religions and Philosophy*. Nairobi, Kenya: East African Educational Publishers.

———. 1975. *Introduction to African Religion*. London: Heinemann Educational.

Menkiti, Ifeanyi A. 2004. "On the Normative Conception of a Person." In *A Companion to African Philosophy*, edited by Kwasi Wiredu, 324–31. Oxford, UK: Blackwell.

Moore, Sally Falk. 2005. *Law and Anthropology: A Reader*. Oxford, UK: Blackwell.

Murungi, John. 2004. "The Question of an African Jurisprudence: Some Hermeneutic Reflections." In *A Companion to African Philosophy*, edited by Kwasi Wiredu, 519–526. Malden, Oxford, Victoria: Blackwell.

———. 2013. *An Introduction to African Legal Philosophy*. Lanham, Maryland: Rowman & Littlefield.

Mwanzi, H. A. 1981. "African Initiatives and Resistance in East Africa, 1880–1914." In *General History of Africa, Volume VII. Africa under Colonial Domination 1880–1935*, edited by Adu A. Boahen, 149–68. Paris: UNESCO, Heinemann, and University of California Press.

Mwenda, Andrew. 2010. "Uganda's Politics of Foreign Aid and Violent Conflict: The Political Uses of the LRA Rebellion." In *The Lord's Resistance Army: Myth and Reality*, edited by Tim Allen and Koen Vlassenroot. London: Zed.

Nyarwath, Oriare. 2019. "Ubuntu and Oruka's Humanitarian View of Punishment." In *Ubuntu and the Reconstitution of Community*, edited by James Ogude, 131–49. Bloomington: Indiana University Press.

Ochola II, MacBaker. 2014. *Spirituality of Reconciliation: A Case Study of Mato Oput within the Context of the Traditional and Cultural Justice System of the Nilotic Acholi/Central Luo People of Northern Uganda*. Africa Justice Project Lecture Series, 1 (1).

Ocholla-Ayayo, A. B. C. 1976. *Traditional Ideology and Ethics among the Southern Luo*. Uppsala, Sweden: Scandinavian Institute of African Studies.

———. 1980. *The Luo Culture*. Wiesbaden, Germany: Franz Steiner.

Odongo, Onyango. "Luo Philosophy of Life." Unpublished manuscript.

Ogude, James, ed. 2019. *Ubuntu and the Reconstitution of Community*. Bloomington: Indiana University Press.

Okumu, Joseph. 2009a. "The Acholi People's Rites of Reconciliation." In *The Examiner* 2, 11–16. Gulu, Uganda: Human Rights Focus.

———. 2009b. "The Acholi People's Rites of Reconciliation—Continued." In *The Examiner* 3, 9–13. Gulu, Uganda: Human Rights Focus.

Onegi, Levis. 2012. "Introduction." In *Where Law Meets Reality: Forging African Transitional Justice*, edited by Moses Chrispus Okello, Chris Dolan, Undine Whande, Nokukhanya Mncwabe, Levis Onegi, and Stephen Oola, 1–3. Cape Town, South Africa: Pambazuka Press.

Oruka, Odera H. 1981. "Four Trends in Current African Philosophy." In *Symposium on "Philosophy in the Present Situation of Africa," Wednesday, August 30, 1978*, edited by Alwin Diemer, 1–7. Wiesbaden, Germany: Franz Steiner.

———. (1976) 1985. *Punishment and Terrorism in Africa*. Nairobi: Kenya Literature Bureau.

———, ed. 1990a. *Sage Philosophy: Indigenous Thinkers and Modern Debate on African Philosophy*. Leiden, Netherlands: E. J. Brill.

———. 1990b. *Trends in African Philosophy*. Nairobi, Kenya: Shirikon.

———, ed. 1991a. *Sage Philosophy: Indigenous Thinkers and Modern Debate on African Philosophy*. Nairobi: ACT Press.

———. 1991b. *The Philosophy of Liberty (An Essay on Political Philosophy)*. Nairobi, Kenya: Standard Textbooks Graphics and Publishing.

———. 1997. *Practical Philosophy: In Search of an Ethical Minimum*. Nairobi, Kenya: East African Educational Publishers.

Pain, Dennis. 1997. *The Bending of the Spears': Producing Consensus for Peace and Development in Northern Uganda*. London: International Alert and Kacoke Madit.

Paine, Clare. 2014. *Ker Kwaro Acholi: A Re-invention of Traditional Authority in Northern Uganda*. MPhil thesis. Aberystwyth University.

p'Bitek, Okot. 1970. *African Religions in Western Scholarship*. Kampala, Uganda: East African Literature Bureau.

———. 1971. *Religion of the Central Luo*. Kampala, Uganda: East African Literature Bureau.

———. (1966) 1972. *Song of Lawino and Song of Ocol: A Lament*. Kampala, Uganda: East African Educational Publishers.

Porter, Holly. 2013. "After Rape. Justice and Social Harmony in Northern Uganda." PhD diss., London School of Economics.

———. 2017. *After Rape: Violence, Justice and Social Harmony in Uganda*. Cambridge, UK: Cambridge University Press.

Porter, Holly, and Anna Macdonald. 2016. "The Trial of Thomas Kwoyelo: Opportunity or Spectre? Reflections on the Ground of the First LRA Prosecution," *Africa* 86 (4): 698–722.

Presbey, Gail. 1998. "Criticisms of Multiparty Democracy: Parallels between Wamba-dia-Wamba and Arendt." *New Political Science* 20 (1): 35–52.

———. 2023. The *Life and Thought of H. Odera Oruka: Pursuing Justice in Africa.* London: Bloomsbury.

Ramose, Mogobe B. 1999. *African Philosophy through Ubuntu.* Harare, Zimbabwe: Mond.

Ricoeur, Paul. 2003. *The Just.* Chicago: University of Chicago Press.

Republic of Uganda. 1967. Judicature Act 1967. Chapter 13.

———. 1995. Constitution of the Republic of Uganda.

———. 2000. The Amnesty Act.

———. 2010. The ICC Act.

Rettová, Alena. 2002. "The Role of African Languages in African Philosophy." *Rue Descartes* 2: 144–46.

Robins, Simon. 2009. "Restorative Approaches to Criminal Justice in Africa: The Case of Uganda." In *The Theory and Practice of Criminal Justice in Africa,* 57–84. African Human Security Initiative. Pretoria, South Africa: ISS.

Samkange, Stanlake John Thompson, and Tommie Marie Samkange. 1980. *Hunhuism or Ubuntuism: A Zimbabwe Indigenous Political Philosophy.* Salisbury, Zimbabwe: Graham.

Schabas, William. 2010. *An Introduction to the International Criminal Court.* Cambridge, UK: Cambridge University Press.

Smiley, Marion. 2022. "Collective Responsibility." *Stanford Encyclopedia of Philosophy.* Last updated December 19, 2022. https://plato.stanford.edu/archives /win2022/entries/collective-responsibility.

Sriram, Chandra Lekha. 2009. Transitional Justice and Peacebuilding. In *Peace Versus Justice? The Dilemma of Transitional Justice in Africa,* edited by Chandra Lekha Sriram and Suren Pillay, 1–17. Cape Town, South Africa: University of KwaZulu-Natal Press.

Sweet, Dennis. 2007. *Heraclitus.* Lanham, MD: University Press of America.

Teitel, Ruti. 2000. *Transitional Justice.* Oxford, UK: Oxford University Press.

———. 2008. "Transitional Justice Genealogy." *Harvard Human Rights Journal* 16: 69–94.

Tempels, Placide. (1945) 1959. *Bantu Philosophy.* Paris: Présence Africaine.

They Slept with Me. 2012. Film. Refugee Law Project.

Titeca, Kristof. 2010. "The Spiritual Order of the LRA." In *The Lord's Resistance Army: Myth and Reality,* edited by Tim Allen and Koen Vlassenroot, 178–219. London: Zed.

Truth and Reconciliation Commission of South Africa. 1998. *Truth and Reconciliation Commission of South Africa Report.* Cape Town, South Africa: Truth and Reconciliation Commission.

UNOHCHR. 2011. *"The Dust Has Not Yet Settled": Victims' Views on the Right to Remedy and Reparation. A Report from the Greater North of Uganda.* Kampala: UN High Commissioner for Human Rights and Uganda Human Rights Commission.

von Benda-Beckmann, Franz. 1984. "Law Out of Context: A Comment on the Creation of Traditional Law Discussion." *Journal of African Law* 28 (1/2): 28–33.
Wiredu, Kwasi. 1980. *Philosophy and an African Culture.* Cambridge, UK:
Cambridge University Press.
———. 1996. *Cultural Universals and Particulars: An African Perspective.* Bloomington: Indiana University Press.
———, ed. 2004. *A Companion to African Philosophy.* Malden, MA: Blackwell.
Wright, A. C. A. 1940. "The Supreme Being among the Acholi of Uganda: Another
Viewpoint." *Uganda Journal* 7 (3): 130–37.

Index

abductees, 1, 3, 31, 33, 41, 50, 95n2; Aboke girls' abduction (October 1996), 28

abila (ancestral shrine), 6–7, 43, 48–49, 70

accountability, 9, 18, 35–36, 40; and collective guilt, 75–77

Acholi (Acholiland): chiefdoms and lineages, 24–25, 32, 69–70, 98nn1, 2; divided into six countries, 25; dual political crises, 27–28; identity, 23, 28, 40, 80–81, 89; internal displacement, 1, 3, 28–29, 33, 95n2, 96n6; not included in British Protectorate, 23; population doubly alienated, 27–28; purity associated with past ways of life, 59–60; Shuuli as name for, 23–24; social stratification, levels of, 35; tradition and philosophy, 11–13. *See also* victims of violence

Acholi Parliamentary Group, 31

Acholi Religious Leaders Peace Initiative (ARLPI), 31, 40–41, 79

Acholi Traditional Justice Mechanisms (ATJMs), 3–8, 33–41; adaptation of, 40–41, 85, 90–91; returnee-welcoming ceremonies, 33–34; and risk of collective guilt, 76; small-scale uses of, 32, 90; and understanding of justice, 22. *See also* community-based collective responsibility; justice

African philosophy, 12–14

African Religions and Philosophy (Mbiti), 70

Agreement on Accountability and Reconciliation (AAR, 2007), 2, 29–30, 34, 95n1

ajwaka (spirit medium), 44, 49, 69–70. *See also* possession

Allen, Tim, 33, 45, 49, 78–79

Amin, Idi, 26

Amnesty Act 2000, 2, 31–32, 40, 83; as "culturally rooted" approach, 57

ancestors, 48; commission of *kir* as offense to, 34–39; *kwo kwaro, kwo macon* as terms for, 11; as sources of moral guidance, 15; and *tumu kir* (cleansing for taboo committed), 34–37, 60. *See also abila* (ancestral shrine); *mato oput* (reconciliation)

Arendt, Hannah, 3, 75–77, 81

Atiak massacre (May 1995), 28

Atkinson, Ronald, 23–24

Awic of Payera (rwot), 25

Baines, Erin, 40

bal (sin), 40

bal ujebu ("contagious sin"), 40, 85

Bantu Philosophy (Tempels), 14, 66

Bantu-speaking Baganda and Banyankole soldiers, 26–27

Banyarwanda, 27

Behrend, Heike, 45, 98–99n3

beings, 97n10; *dano* (human being), 63–65; nonliving and nonhuman entities, 8, 42, 47, 67. *See also* personhood

Bidima, Jean Godefroy, 71

Bigombe, Betty, 3

BENEDETTA LANFRANCHI is a researcher at the University of Bayreuth under the European Research Council Consolidator Grant "Philosophy and Genre: Creating a Textual Basis for African Philosophy," for which she is writing her second monograph titled *Digital Intellectuals: Fighting for Freedom in Uganda*. She is also Adjunct Assistant Professor at the American University of Rome (AUR) where she teaches ethics, political thought, and international relations theory. She is coeditor of *Critical Conversations in African Philosophy: Asixoxe— Let's Talk*.

For Indiana University Press

Sabrina Black, Editorial Assistant
Tony Brewer, Artist and Book Designer
Anna Francis, Assistant Acquisitions Editor
Anna Garnai, Production Coordinator
Katie Huggins, Production Manager
Alyssa Nicole Lucas, Marketing and Publicity Manager
David Miller, Lead Project Manager/Editor
Bethany Mowry, Acquisitions Editor
Dan Pyle, Online Publishing Manager
Jennifer L. Wilder, Senior Artist and Book Designer